PRIORITIES FOR LIVING
Series

MAKING YOUR WORK COUNT FOR GOD

➤ *How to find meaning and joy in your work*

THOMAS NELSON PUBLISHERS
Nashville • Atlanta • London • Vancouver

◆ Contents ◆

◆ *Acknowledgments* ◆

Chapter 2: Song lyrics on page 29 are from "God Wants a Holy People," by Ken and Tink Abraham (Nashville, TN: Evergreen Music Group, 1977). Used by permission.

Chapter 5: The quotes by Mother Teresa on pages 68 and 72 are taken from *Blessed Are You* by Eileen Egan and Kathleen Egan (Ann Arbor, MI: Servant Publications, 1992), 15–56. Used by permission.

Chapter 7: For the Tams' complete story (page 99), see *God Owns My Business* by Stanley Tam (Dallas: Word Books, 1969). Used by permission.

Unless otherwise noted, stories about persons in this book are fictitious. Any resemblance to actual persons or incidents is coincidental.

Narrative and questions written by Ken Abraham.

✦ *Foreword* ✦

The *Priorities for Living* series has been created to offer you friendly companions for discovering the relevance of God's Word and for applying it to everyday life. The series addresses a variety of issues that believers face in today's world. It contains a wide selection of articles and relevant Scripture from *The Word In Life Study Bible*™, which allow these workbooks to be used as independent tools for individual or group study. Each workbook in the series is based on a theme that has been developed in *The Word In Life Study Bible*™.

It has been said that Scripture was not written merely to be read, but to change lives. James urges us to be "doers of the word, and not hearers only" (James 1:22). The purpose of God's Word is to help us become more like Jesus Christ by making the Word of God part of our lives. *The Word In Life Study Bible*™ was created to help us discover how to relate God's Word to the world we live in.

Applying biblical truth today is not always easy—especially since the Bible was written thousands of years ago. Many wonder how the Bible can be connected to today's complex society. However, as you explore the pages of this book, you will discover how surprisingly relevant God's Word is to your daily life and how you can make a difference in your world.

• *Life's Dirtiest Word* •

Of all the four-letter words in the English language, one of the worst you can say to many people is W-O-R-K. That's right, work. *Some people hate it. Others become fatigued at the mere thought of it. Many avoid it completely.*

Yet, work is a spiritual subject. The Bible mentions it more than 150 times, almost always favorably. In Scripture, work—striving toward a goal or some purposeful, constructive activity—is portrayed as a positive part of our lives. Work is not meaningless drudgery. It is fulfilling and, in most cases, rewarding either financially, physically, emotionally, intellectually, or spiritually.

Occasionally Christians are tempted to think that they are exempt from work. They assume that they will eventually be going to heaven, so what's the point in working up a sweat while they are here on earth? Either that, or they adopt an attitude of indifference toward their work because, in their minds, the mundane work world has little eternal value. But that is simply not true. Your work matters to God; He is extremely interested not only in what you do as your work, but also in how and why you do it.

What? No Retirement?

It may surprise you to learn that Christians will continue to work in heaven. Sorry to dispel any ideas you may have about sitting around heaven, strumming a harp. That picture may emanate from some painter's fertile imagination, but it is not how Scripture describes heaven. The Bible indicates that work will be a meaningful part of our eternal existence.

The apostle Paul once confronted a few folks who were so heavenly-minded that they were no earthly good. Concerning such folks, the apostle admonished, "If anyone will not work, neither shall he eat" (2 Thess. 3:10). Many of the new believers to whom Paul wrote were so excited about the possibility of Christ's returning soon, they lost their enthusiasm for everyday work and tended to live off their friends and families. The misguided believers spent most of their time as busybodies. Their attitude was: Why work when Jesus is coming any day now?

Obviously, the apostle was opposed to sponging off other people while waiting for the Lord's return. Paul just says, "Get to work!" He tells misguided believers to stop being disorderly and undisciplined. Quit being a busybody and get your body busy (2 Thess. 3:11).

The early Christian "welfare system" took excellent care of widows, orphans, and others who were in need, but the early church allowed no place for lazy, lackadaisical loafers. The biblical standard was this: If you are physically able, then you'd better be working at something. Idleness is not allowed in the kingdom of God.

Paul set the example for us. To meet his own needs and to avoid being a burden to the churches to whom he ministered, Paul worked at what we might call an "ordinary" job. He supported himself by making tents during many of his missionary travels.

Up with People

Work does wonders for your self-image. It is not how much you get paid, or even if you get paid, that counts. The most important aspect of work is what it does for you on the inside; it gives you a sense of accomplishment, significance, and dignity.

But please understand that your work does not define your value as a person. Many people have been duped into believing that their worth is determined by what they can contribute to society. The idea is this: As long as you function as a well-greased cog in society's machine and contribute to the good of others, you have value as a person. But if (actually, when) you can no longer perform properly, you become expendable. Such thinking is unbiblical.

Your life has intrinsic value to God regardless of the legacy you leave to society. Success in God's eyes is not measured by dollars, plaques, gold watches, monuments, or buildings bearing your name. You are important to God because you exist.

And because God values you, He has called you to work with Him in the world. Scripture says, "For we are His workmanship, created in Christ Jesus for good works, which God prepared beforehand that we should walk in them" (Eph. 2:10). As such, God asks you to represent Christ in your workplace, and, to put it another way, He asks you to re-present Jesus to the world around you.

Where Is My Workplace?

Obviously, your job—the place where you earn your income—is your workplace. On the other hand, for millions of homemakers who do not receive financial remuneration for their long, arduous hours of work, the workplace may be their home, the local Parent-Teacher Organization, the Post Office, the Little League field, ballet or music lessons, the grocery store, or an endless variety of other locations in which they regularly interact with the world.

Many retired persons and volunteer workers may not make money in their workplace, but they put in as much time, energy, and heartfelt effort as if they were the highest-paid employees in a company.

Clearly then, your workplace can be wherever you spend the majority of your time interacting with society. It may be in the corner office on the top floor of your company, or it might be on a construction site, or it may be taking your turn in the neighborhood watch program. Your workplace also includes the people who surround you on a daily basis, as well as the issues and interests that touch their lives.

It is into the workplace that your heavenly Father invites you to represent Jesus. He calls you to take His Word into your world and to live out your Christian life with such honesty, integrity, and transparency that everyone around you can watch His Word working in you. By observing your life, they can see "Christ in you, the hope of glory" (Col. 1:27), and say, "Now I understand what it means to be a Christian, and that's the kind of person I want to be!"

How to Use This Book

This workbook is designed to help you live out your walk with Christ in the world. Although the book is directed to you, the individual reader, and is primarily intended as a private volume in which you can record your personal responses, it can also be used as a group study and discussion guide. If the workbook is used for group study, each member of the group should have his or her own book to ensure privacy. A Leader's Guide is included in the back of the book.

Each lesson is self-contained and is made up of thought-provoking articles, relevant Scriptures, and practical applications. To gain the maximum benefit from your workbook, please read all of the material in each chapter. Throughout the book, you will be invited to write your responses to specific questions based upon what you have read. Many of your responses will involve your personal thoughts, feelings, experiences, and areas of your life in which you sense the need to improve.

Obviously, you could answer the questions mentally and then move on to the next subject, but it is extremely helpful to put your answers on paper. As you record your responses, you will begin to think through why you feel and believe the way you do. More important, you will have a written record of some matters about which God may be speaking to you concerning your attitudes and actions.

When you write your responses, express your thoughts and feelings as freely and honestly as possible. Don't worry about spelling, grammar, or sentence structure. Don't try to impress anyone with your answers. No teacher or critic is looking over your shoulder, waiting to correct you if you record the wrong response. In fact, most of your responses cannot be considered right or wrong since they are simply reflections of your own thoughts and feelings. No tests will be given at the end of the book; it's a course you're sure to pass with flying colors!

When using your workbook, find a quiet, comfortable place where you can be free to express your thoughts and feelings without interruption. Allow yourself plenty of time to read each chapter carefully, then thoughtfully respond to the questions. Seek the Lord's guidance concerning areas in which He may want you to change.

Remember, you may not be able to change many of the circumstances surrounding your workplace. You can't change your coworkers. But you can change your own attitudes and actions, and that will make your time with this workbook a rich and worthwhile experience. Happy working!

"BUT IT'S JUST *WORK*"

Whew! Thank God it's Friday," Steve whispered as he slumped into a seat next to Renee and Neil, who were eating lunch at a small table in the employees' cafeteria. Steve pulled his chair up closer to his coworkers and a broad smile spread across his face. "A few more hours and I'm out of here!"

"Did you have a rough week?" asked Neil.

"Naw, no more than usual."

"You must have a big weekend planned," Renee coaxed.

"I sure do," gushed Steve. "I just can't wait until our choir concert on Saturday night. Our choir is such an incredible group to be involved with! Everyone's so talented and friendly. I'm so glad I joined; the choir provides an important part of the worship service. Our hard work really matters."

"But Steve," Renee protested, "your work here is important, too."

"That's right," Neil agreed. "You are one of the best in your department. We need you around here."

"Thanks," Steve blushed a bit at the compliment, "but it's all so meaningless. These people around here don't care about me. And they sure don't seem to care about God!"

"Aren't you happy with your work?" Renee asked.

"Oh, sure; but it's just *work*. It's what I do to put food on the table, and clothes on the kids, and some money in the bank. I make a more important contribution at church."

Renee replied quietly, "Well, Steve, I want to make my work count, too. But I feel my workplace is my mission field."

• • • • • • • • •

Like Steve, you may have some misconceptions about the meaning and value of your work. You are not alone. Myths, mistakes, and blatantly unbiblical concepts about work abound.

Steve's conversation with Renee and Neil reveals several of his misconceptions. Before reading the article "Workplace Myths," scan their conversation again, find some of the more common myths about the nature and value of work, and list them below.

_____

_____

_____

_____

_____

Now, let's stick some pins in those mythological balloons that have been floating around your workplace. Be prepared! Some of the "pops" you experience as we expose these myths may shake up your status quo. That's okay. Keep in mind that sometimes God has to jostle us a bit to jolt us out of our jaded assumptions about our world.

WORKPLACE MYTHS

Paul called himself one of God's "fellow workers" (1 Cor. 3:9). In a similar way, every one of us is a coworker with God. Yet certain distorted views of work have taken on mythical proportions in Western culture. They've had devastating effects on both the people and the message of Christ. Here's a sampling of these pernicious myths, along with a few points of rebuttal:

Myth: Church work is the only work that has any real spiritual value.
In other words, everyday work in the "secular" world counts for nothing of lasting value. Only "sacred" work matters to God.

Fact: Christianity makes no distinction between the "sacred" and the "secular."

All of life is to be lived under Christ's lordship. So when it comes to work, all work has essential value to God, and workers will answer to Him for how they have carried out the work He has given to them (1 Cor. 3:13).

Myth: The heroes of the faith are ministers and missionaries. "Lay" workers remain second-class.
This follows from the previous idea. If "sacred" work is the only work with eternal value, then "sacred workers" (clergy) are the most valuable workers. The best that "laypeople" can do is to support the clergy and engage in "ministry" during their spare hours.

Fact: God has delegated His work to everybody, not just clergy.

Among the main characters of Scripture are ranchers, farmers, fishermen, vintners, ironworkers, carpenters, tentmakers, textile manufacturers, public officials, construction supervisors and workers, military personnel, financiers, physicians, judges, tax collectors, musicians, sculptors, dancers, poets, and writers, among others. Nowhere does God view these people or their work as "second class" or "secular." Rather, their work accomplishes God's

continued

work in the world. As we do our work each day, we reflect the very image of God, who is a working God. He spent six days working on the creation (Gen. 1:31—2:3), so we merely follow God's example when we work five or six days out of the week.

Myth: Work is a part of the curse.

According to this belief, God punished Adam and Eve for their sin by laying the burden of work on them: "In the sweat of your face you shall eat bread till you return to the ground" (Gen. 3:19). That's why work is so often drudgery, and why the workplace is driven by greed and selfishness.

Fact: Work is a gift from God.

The Bible never calls work a curse, but rather a gift from God (Eccl. 3:13; 5:18–19). God gave Adam and Eve work to do long before they ever sinned (Gen. 2:15), and He commends and commands work long after the fall (Gen. 9:1–7; Col. 3:23; 1 Thess. 4:11).

Myth: God is no longer involved in His creation.

For many, if not most, modern-day workers, God is irrelevant in the workplace. He may exist, but He has little to do with everyday matters of the work world. These people don't care much about what God does, and they assume He doesn't care much about what they do, either.

Fact: God remains intimately connected with both His world and its workers.

Scripture knows nothing of a detached Creator. He actively holds the creation together (Col. 1:16–17) and works toward its ultimate restoration from sin (John 5:17; Rom. 8:18–25). He uses the work of people to accomplish many of His purposes. Indeed, believers ultimately work for Christ as their Boss. He takes an active

interest in how they do their work (Titus 2:9–10).

Myth: You only go around once in life—so you better make the most of it!

This is the "heaven can wait" perspective. Here-and-now is what matters; it's where the excitement is. Heaven is just a make-believe world of gold-paved streets and never-ending choirs. Boring! Why not enjoy your reward right now? Go for it!

Fact: God is saving the greatest rewards for eternity—and work will be among them.

Scripture doesn't offer much detail about life after death, but it does promise a future society remade by God where work goes on—without the sweat, toil, pain, or futility of the curse (Is. 65:17–25; Rev. 22:2–5). And as for the question of rewards, God plans to hand out rewards for how believers have spent their lives—including their work (1 Cor. 3:9–15).

Myth: The most important day of the week is Friday.

"Thank God it's Friday!" the secular work ethic cries. Because work is drudgery, weekends are for escaping—and catching up. There's no idea of a Sabbath, just a couple of days of respite from the grinding routine.

Fact: God wants us to pursue cycles of meaningful work and restorative rest.

A biblical view of work places a high value on rest. God never intended us to work seven days a week. He still invites us to join Him in a day of rest, renewal, and celebration. That restores us to go back to our work with a sense of purpose and mission. "Thank God it's Monday!" we can begin to say. ◆

1 Corinthians 3:5–9

[5]Who then is Paul, and who is Apollos, but ministers through whom you believed, as the Lord gave to each one? [6]I planted, Apollos watered, but God gave the increase. [7]So then neither he who plants is anything, nor he who waters, but God who gives the increase. [8]Now he who plants and he who waters are one, and each one will receive his own reward according to his own labor.

[9]For we are God's fellow workers; you are God's field, you are God's building.

——◆ Attitude Check ◆——

Let's identify where you are right now in your attitude toward your work. Place a check mark by those statements that apply to you.

_____ Each day of work is a fresh challenge to me.
_____ I feel that if I were doing something "more spiritual" my work would be more valuable to God.
_____ I hardly know any of my coworkers.
_____ Nobody at my workplace really cares about me.
_____ I feel uncomfortable around my non-Christian coworkers.
_____ I rarely talk about God at work.
_____ I'm afraid to think too highly of my work for fear I will slip into sinful pride.
_____ God is pleased with the tasks I perform at my workplace.
_____ My work is making a difference in the world around me.
_____ I am pleased with my work.

Complete the following sentence: My attitude toward my workplace could be better if

_____

_____

The Church versus the World

1. From where do you suppose notions of "church work" and "secular work" came?

_____

_____

2. Complete the following sentences:
When I am involved in "spiritual work," I feel _____

_____

The main reason I like (or dislike) my work is _____

_____

_____

I would be happier and feel more fulfilled investing my time in _____

_____

_____

Where Is God at Work?

1. What will be the major difference between work in heaven and work in the world?

_____

_____

2. The chances of God using me as His witness in my workplace are

_____ excellent
_____ good
_____ possible, but not probable
_____ poor
_____ none

3a. Impacting your workplace for Christ requires more than merely making glib comments about God. Displaying Christian values, such as honesty, integrity, fairness, discipline, and hard work, is an equally important way to show others Christ. What would it take for your coworkers to recognize God in your workplace?

_____

_____

_____

3b. List some practical things you can do to help your coworkers' recognition of God in your workplace become a reality.

_____

_____

_____

——◆ Coworking with God ◆——

Look again at 1 Corinthians 3:9 on page 4. Notice that it says, "We are God's fellow workers." What an honor! But what do you think it means? What are some down-to-earth ways you can labor with your heavenly Father?

_____

_____

_____

_____

_____

The fact that "you are God's field, you are God's building" (3:9) should give you an incredible sense of worth. Almighty God is creating a great work in and through you. He is building His kingdom together with you. That means your work has immediate, temporal value, as well as eternal significance. Unfortunately, the fellow in the following story may not have understood this.

◆ ◆ ◆ ◆ ◆ ◆ ◆ ◆ ◆

Nobody knew for sure why the disheveled drunk died. Nobody knew his name. Nobody cared. He just didn't matter.

Finally, a friend found him . . . at the morgue. The coroner gave the friend all of his homeless buddy's belongings—a filthy, tattered coat with thirty-eight cents in one pocket, and a crumpled piece of paper in the other. On the scrap of paper was scrawled, "Dear friends and gentle hearts."

The line sounded almost like the lyrics to a song, and it might have been had the drunken derelict lived a little longer. After all, the man was a songwriter.

Today, the whole world knows his memorable songs such as "Beautiful Dreamer,"

"Camptown Races," "Jeanie With the Light Brown Hair," "Old Folks at Home," and "Oh Susanna!" But back then, his naked body was found with his head badly bruised and his throat slit, and nobody cared that one of the all-time-great American composers lay bleeding to death in the gutter. Stephen Foster was dead at thirty-eight years of age, and nobody cared.

Perhaps this great songwriter simply needed to know that he mattered to God and so did his work. If he had this reassurance, he may not have died like he did.

Perhaps you have experienced that gnawing feeling that who you are and what you do really does not make much dif-

ference one way or the other. You believe that God can do anything, but do you really believe that God can do anything through *you?*

Yet, from the beginning of time God has delegated His authority to human beings and has given us the incredible privilege of representing Him. God gave Adam and Eve a mandate to rule over the earth, and that mandate has never been rescinded. Despite man's sin, God's command remained intact. Granted, throughout history misguided men and women have often twisted this command to rule and made it into selfish excuses for raping His planet of its natural resources, taking unfair advantage of other people, and using God's precious treasures to build their own empires, rather than His.

Nevertheless, God's mandate remains. He still wants to extend His rule over the world through you. ◆

◆ ◆ ◆ ◆ ◆ ◆ ◆ ◆ ◆

PEOPLE AT WORK

*D*o you know that your job is an extension of Christ's rule over the world? Hebrews 2:7 cites Psalm 8:4–6 to support its point that Christ is Lord of the earth. But Psalm 8 also shows that God has given people authority over the world. It looks back to the Creation account (Gen. 1:26–30), where God created humanity in His image to be His coworkers in overseeing the creation. Consider what that means:*

(1) You bear the very image of God. Like Him, you are a person, which means you have dignity and value. You matter. Who you are and what you do are significant. God has created you for a reason, which gives your life ultimate meaning and purpose.

(2) You are created to be a worker. God is a worker, and since you are made in His image, your work expresses something of who He is and what He wants done in the world. Work (activity that advances your own well-being or that of someone else, or that manages the creation in a godly way) reflects the work that God does. That means your work has dignity and value. It matters to God.

(3) You are God's coworker. Genesis 1:26–30 makes it clear that God wants people to manage the world. He gives us authority to "subdue" the earth—to cultivate and develop it, bring it under our control, use it to meet our needs, explore its wonders, and learn to cooperate with its natural laws. He also gives us "dominion" over every plant and animal for similar purposes.

Your job can help accomplish that mandate, as you use your God-given skills and opportunities. He views your work as having not only dignity, but purpose and direction as well. He wants you to accomplish meaningful tasks as you labor with a Christlike work ethic. Ultimately, He wants you to bring Him glory as a faithful manager of the resources and responsibilities He has placed under your control. By approaching work from this perspective, you can find fulfillment and motivation as a partner with God Himself. ◆

Hebrews 2:6–8

⁶But one testified in a certain place, saying:

> "What is man that You are mindful of him,
> Or the son of man that You take care of him?
> 7 You have made him a little lower than the angels;
> You have crowned him with glory and honor,
> And set him over the works of Your hands.
> 8 You have put all things in subjection under his feet."

For in that He put all in subjection under him, He left nothing *that is* not put under him. But now we do not yet see all things put under him.

1. Imagine that you are going to be the president for one day. What would you do during your twenty-four-hour reign over the United States? (For instance: I'd establish world peace.)

_____

_____

_____

2. In what ways could your work be an extension of Christ's rule over the world?

_____

_____

_____

3. What does the writer to the Hebrews mean when he says God made man "a little lower than the angels" (2:7)?

_____

_____

_____

4. How does God's command to manage His world relate to environmental and ecological issues?

_____

_____

_____

—◆ Your Work, Your Witness ◆—

Bob was studying his Bible diligently and enjoying it thoroughly. He was getting paid, however, by an automaker to build automobiles on the assembly line. Occasionally Bob became so intrigued with something he was reading in God's Word, he missed a car going by on the line. *Oh well,* he'd think. *One of the quality control people will catch it and repair it down the line.* At other times, Bob did shabby work because of his eagerness to get back to his Bible study.

Bob frequently engaged his coworkers in discussions about his religious convictions. He simply wanted to express his faith. But his boss wanted Bob to build quality cars.

The inevitable happened. A company foreman finally lost his patience with Bob's poor performance and fired him.

Bob cried foul play. He considered his termination to be religious persecution. "It's not fair," he pleaded with the foreman. "I just wanted to be a good Christian witness to the people on the line."

"Your best witness around here," the foreman retorted, "is quality work!" ◆

◆ ◆ ◆ ◆ ◆ ◆ ◆ ◆ ◆

Who do you think was more pleasing to God?

_____ Bob
_____ The foreman

If you were Bob, what would you have done differently?

_____

_____

If you were the foreman, what would you have done differently?

_____

_____

Frequently, the best witness you can have for Christ in your workplace is to do excellent work, regardless of the apparent importance of the task. Otherwise, your glowing words about Jesus will fall upon deaf ears.

You must establish a reputation as a conscientious worker with your boss and fellow workers so they can have absolute assurance that when you are assigned a responsibility, it will be done to the best of your ability. The Christian in the workplace should not need someone constantly looking over his shoulder, checking to make sure that he is doing the job he is being paid to do.

Why? As a Christian, you have a responsibility: "Whatever you do in word or deed, do all in the name of the Lord Jesus" (Col. 3:17). In other words, you are representing Jesus on the job. You are not merely working for a paycheck or a pat on the back. You are working to please the Lord.

Whether your work skills are rare and highly regarded in the eyes of the world, or they are routine and ignored by the masses is not the issue. Whether millions of people watch you work (as in the case of a professional athlete, politician, or celebrity), or you work in obscure, lonely isolation (such as a forest ranger, lab technician, or a live-in companion for a senior citizen), your commitment to excellence should not vary. Scripture says, "Whatever you do, do it heartily, as to the Lord and not to men, knowing that from the Lord you will receive the reward of the inheritance; for you serve the Lord Christ" (Col. 3:23–24).

In that sense, your work is an expression of your devotion to God. A busy wife and mother posted these words above her sink: Divine Services Held Here Three Times Daily. The most tedious, tasteless task can be an act of worship when you do it "heartily, as to the Lord."

THE SPIRITUALITY OF EVERYDAY WORK

What does Colossians 3:1–2 imply about everyday work? Is it possible to hold a "secular" job and still "seek those things which are above" rather than "things on the earth"? Or would it be better to quit one's job and go into the ministry?

The issue here is *spirituality*, the capacity to know, experience, and respond to God. How is it possible to bring spirituality into "secular" work? Consider:

If Christ is Lord over all of life, then He must be Lord over work, too. Colossians 3 does not distinguish between the sacred and the secular, but between the life that Christ offers, (the "things above") and its alternative—spiritual death apart from Him (the "things on the earth"). This is clear from the preceding context (2:20) and the rest of chapter 3: "earthly" things include fornication, uncleanness, passion, etc. (vv. 5, 8); the "things above" include tender mercies, kindness, humility, etc. (vv. 12–15). Spirituality has to do with conduct and character, not just vocation.

It also has to do with the lordship of Christ. Christ is Lord over all of creation (1:15–18). Therefore, He is Lord over work. Whatever we do for work, we should do it "in the name of the Lord Jesus" (v. 17), that is, with a concern for His approval and in a manner that honors Him. In fact, Paul specifically addresses two categories of workers—slaves (v. 22–25) and masters (4:1)—in this manner.

The Spirit empowers us to live and work with Christlikeness. Spirituality has to do with character and conduct, regardless of where we work. Christ gives the Holy Spirit to help us live in a way that pleases Him (Gal. 5:16–25). That has enormous implications for how we do our jobs, our "workstyle" (Titus 2:9–10).

Furthermore, Scripture calls us "temples" of the Holy Spirit (1 Cor. 6:19). An intriguing image: In Exodus 31 and 35, the Spirit enabled Hebrew workers to use their skills in stonecutting, carpentry, lapidary arts, and so on to construct a beautiful, functional house of worship. In an even greater way, we can

continued

continued

expect the Spirit to enable us to use our God-given skills and abilities to bring glory to God.

God values our work even when the product has no eternal value. A common measure of the significance of a job is its perceived value from the eternal perspective. Will the work "last"? Will it "really count" for eternity? The assumption is that God values work for eternity, but not work for the here and now.

By this measure, the work of ministers and missionaries has eternal value because it deals with the spiritual, eternal needs of people. By contrast, the work of the shoe salesman, bank teller, or typist has only limited value, because it meets only earthly needs. Implication: that kind of work doesn't really "count" to God.

But this way of thinking overlooks several important truths:

(1) God Himself has created a world which is time-bound and temporary (2 Pet. 3:10–11). Yet He values His work, declaring it to be "very good," good by its very nature (Gen. 1:31; Ps. 119:68; Acts 14:17).

(2) God promises rewards to people in everyday jobs, based on their attitude and conduct (Eph. 6:7–9; Col. 3:23—4:1).

(3) God cares about the everyday needs of people as well as their spiritual needs. He cares whether people have food, clothing, shelter, and so forth.

(4) God cares about people, who will enter eternity. To the extent that a job serves the needs of people, He values it because He values people. ◆

Colossians 3:1–4

[1]If then you were raised with Christ, seek those things which are above, where Christ is, sitting at the right hand of God. [2]Set your mind on things above, not on things on the earth. [3]For you died, and your life is hidden with Christ in God. [4]When Christ *who is* our life appears, then you also will appear with Him in glory.

1a. Colossians 3:2 instructs you to "set your mind on things above, not on things on the earth." What are some of the "things above" upon which you are to concentrate?

_____

_____

_____

1b. What are some of the things in your workplace that could possibly distract you from your "heavenly priorities"?

_____

_____

_____

_____

2. If Jesus were working where you work, what would He do differently from what you are currently doing?

_____

_____

_____

_____

3. What aspects of Christ's character would be especially attractive to your coworkers? (For instance, His integrity, love, and peace.)

_____

_____

_____

_____

_____

4a. In what areas of your life do you sense a deep need for Christ's character to be made more real?

_____

_____

_____

_____

4b. How would Christ's character in you affect your conduct in your workplace?

_____

_____

_____

_____

——◆ It's a Living ◆——

Just for fun, rate the following careers according to how you view their "spirituality," with number one being the career with the most spiritual value and number eight being the one with the least. If you view the careers as equal, then rate them the same.

_____ Rock Star   _____ Pastor
_____ Missionary   _____ Lawyer
_____ Salesperson   _____ Teacher
_____ Construction Worker   _____ Farmer

Now read "Are Some Jobs More Important Than Others?" and let's check God's priority list.

ARE SOME JOBS MORE IMPORTANT THAN OTHERS?

Does a hierarchy of gifts (1 Cor. 12:28–31) mean God values some jobs more than others? Judging by popular opinion, one might conclude that He does. In fact, for centuries Christians have subscribed to a subtle yet powerful hierarchy of vocations.

In our culture, that hierarchy tends to position clergy (missionaries and evangelists, pastors and priests) at the top, members of the "helping professions" (doctors and nurses, teachers and educators, social workers) next, and "secular" workers (business executives, salespeople, factory laborers and farmers) at the bottom.

So what determines the spiritual value of a job? How does God assign significance? The hierarchy assumes sacred and secular distinctions, and assigns priority to the sacred. But does God view vocations that way? No . . .

All legitimate work matters to God. *God Himself is a worker. In fact, human occupations find their origin in His work to create the world (Ps. 8:6–8). Work is a gift from Him to meet the needs of people and the creation.*

God creates people to carry out specific kinds of work. *God uniquely designs each of us, fitting us for certain kinds of tasks. He distributes skills, abilities, interests, and personalities among us so that we can carry out His work*

continued

continued

in the world. That work includes "spiritual" tasks, but also extends to health, education, agriculture, business, law, communication, the arts, and so on.

God cares more about character and conduct than occupational status. *Paul's teaching in this passage is about gifts, not vocations. At the time Paul wrote it, there were few if any "professional" clergy in the church. Paul himself was a tentmaker by occupation, along with his friends, Aquila and Priscilla (1 Cor. 16:19; Rom. 16:3–5). Other church leaders practiced a wide variety of professions and trades. God may assign rank among the spiritual gifts; but there's no indication that He looks at vocations that way.*

Furthermore, Scripture says there is something more important than gifts, "a more excellent way" (1 Cor. 12:31). Chapter 13 reveals it to be the way of Christlike love and character. Implication: If you want status in God's economy, excel at love, no matter what you do for work. Love has the greatest value to God (1 Cor. 13:13; Matt. 22:35–40). ◆

---

 1 Corinthians 12:15–31

[15]If the foot should say, "Because I am not a hand, I am not of the body," is it therefore not of the body? [16]And if the ear should say, "Because I am not an eye, I am not of the body," is it therefore not of the body? [17]If the whole body *were* an eye, where *would be* the hearing? If the whole *were* hearing, where *would be* the smelling? [18]But now God has set the members, each one of them, in the body just as He pleased. [19]And if they *were* all one member, where *would* the body be?

[20]But now indeed *there are* many members, yet one body. [21]And the eye cannot say to the hand, "I have no need of you"; nor again the head to the feet, "I have no need of you." [22]No, much rather, those members of the body which seem to be weaker are necessary. [23]And those *members* of the body which we think to be less honorable, on these we bestow greater honor; and our unpresentable *parts* have greater modesty, [24]but our presentable *parts* have no need. But God composed the body, having given greater honor to that *part* which lacks it, [25]that there should be no schism in the body, but *that* the members should have the same care for one another. [26]And if one member suffers, all the members suffer with *it*; or if one member is honored, all the members rejoice with *it*.

[27]Now you are the body of Christ, and members individually. [28]And God has appointed these in the church: first apostles, second prophets, third teachers, after that miracles, then gifts of healings, helps, administrations, varieties of tongues. [29]Are all apostles? *Are* all prophets? *Are* all teachers? *Are* all workers of miracles? [30]Do all have gifts of healings? Do all speak with tongues? Do all interpret? [31]But earnestly desire the best gifts. And yet I show you a more excellent way.

1a. Suppose your entire body were one giant eye; you would probably have great vision, but how could you hear? Or, what if you really were "all ears"? How would you taste your food? What if your body were one big nose . . . no, you don't even want to think about that one! Fortunately, God brilliantly designed you to have many "members," which are all part of the same body.

In 1 Corinthians 12:15–27, the apostle Paul paints a humorous picture of the body of

Christ before driving home his main point. List several principles from this passage you regard as important in respect to your attitude toward your workplace.

_____

_____

_____

1b. What do you feel is Paul's main point in this passage?

_____

_____

_____

2. How does this passage relate to the hierarchy of gifts mentioned in 1 Corinthians 12:28–31?

_____

_____

_____

_____

3. What is the "more excellent way" Paul alludes to in verse 31?

_____

_____

_____

4. What are some specific ways your living out "the more excellent way" might make a difference in your character and conduct at your workplace? (For instance: I will respond with kind words the next time my work is criticized.)

_____

_____

_____

_____

──◆ Taking Inventory ◆──

As you better understand how highly God values your work, you will find a sense of purpose that far surpasses the satisfaction you receive from getting a paycheck, or even the "warm fuzzies" you feel when you receive the appreciation of your superiors or the respect of your peers. Knowing that your work matters to God gives you that extra incentive to get out of bed each morning, cope with a car that won't start, fight the traffic or a variety of other obstacles, and still walk into your workplace with a smile on your face.

Why? Because you know that you are not just killing time. You are not merely making a living. You are helping God meet the needs of the world. You are faithfully managing the resources and responsibilities that He has placed under your control. Service replaces selfishness as your motivation for what you do. No wonder a proper biblical perspective about the nature and value of your work reinforces your dignity and self-respect! Just knowing that your work honors God puts a lilt in your step and lifts your spirit. What a privilege to be working with God!

Of course, with privilege comes responsibility. Since you represent Jesus at your job, you have an even greater responsibility to do honest, quality work. Your work should earn you the right to be heard when you speak of Jesus Christ in your workplace.

But be forewarned: being a Christian in the workplace isn't always easy. Nor is it always popular. Your desire to please Christ may often clash with the status quo in the workplace, especially if the majority of your coworkers are not Christians. To survive and thrive in such an environment, you will need to think through some nitty-gritty such as:

- *Who is the real boss?*
- *Who gets the credit (or the blame)?*
- *What is a fair relationship between labor and management?*
- *And, most importantly, who really cares about what goes on in your workplace?*

In the next chapter, we'll look more closely at these questions. Get ready. Some of your discoveries might surprise you!

A COMMITMENT TO EXCELLENCE

Susan, be sure to turn out the lights and don't forget to empty the garbage before you leave. At least be good for something," Dr. Landers said loudly enough for all the other employees in the office to hear. Dr. Landers arrogantly swept past Susan's desk on his way out of the office. "Oh," Landers said, stopping short of the exit and turning back toward Susan, "and if those reports are not on my desk first thing in the morning, don't bother coming to work. You will no longer be employed here!" Dr. Landers slammed the door behind him.

"What did I do to deserve this sort of treatment?" lamented Susan, as she blinked back the tears. At one time, Susan and Dr. Landers had enjoyed a cordial, professional relationship. But lately, for no obvious reason, her boss had begun treating Susan with contempt. He frequently spoke rudely to her in front of fellow employees, making snide remarks about her work, ridiculing her professionalism, and insulting her intelligence.

Pick! Pick! Pick! That's all her boss ever did. Nothing Susan did was ever good enough in Landers' estimation. Whenever she suggested an idea that might help things run more smoothly in the office, Landers simply smiled condescendingly. Then, in a disdainful tone of voice, he dismissed her ideas without even considering them.

Although Susan possessed better academic and professional credentials than any of her coworkers, her boss consistently assigned her mundane chores, such as turning out the office lights and emptying the garbage. It seemed to Susan that Dr. Landers was purposely attempting to discourage her to the point of quitting.

But Susan needed this job too much to quit. Her husband was unemployed, and with three children at home Susan felt she couldn't afford to simply pack up and leave Dr. Landers' office. Times were tough and good-paying jobs were difficult to find. She gritted her teeth, prayed a lot, and did her best to be kind, respectful, and conscientious about her work.

Nevertheless, it was getting tougher by the day and Susan wondered how much more she could take.

◆ ◆ ◆ ◆ ◆ ◆ ◆ ◆ ◆

If you were Susan's best friend, what would you suggest she do?

Almost everyone who has spent any time in the workplace has a horror story about a boss who was a creep. What can you do when your boss acts like a jerk? What should your attitude be if your boss is rude, domineering, unfair, oppressive, unappreciative, or engages in flagrantly non-Christian conduct in the workplace? And why should you even care?

Tough questions. Take a look at the article "Who's the Boss?" and see if you can find some practical answers.

WHO'S THE BOSS?

He had a menial, dead-end job. They assigned him tasks that no one else wanted—the "dumb-work," the dirty work, the dangerous work. They called him out at all hours of the day and night to satisfy the whims of his supervisors. He had little hope for advancement. In fact, he'd be lucky just to keep his job; plenty of others stood in line, ready to replace him. Whether he even lived or died mattered little. He was a first-century Roman slave.

Yet he mattered to God, and his work mattered, too. In writing to this lowly worker (Col. 3:22–24), Paul redefined his occupational status: he was not just a Roman slave, he was an employee of Christ the Lord! That makes all the difference.

So it is for any Christian in the workplace. You may work for a giant multinational corporation or a mom-'n-pop pizza parlor. You may have 15 levels of bureaucracy over you, or be self-employed. It doesn't matter. Ultimately, Christ is your Boss. Consider what that means:

Christ gives you work to do. *Work is a gift from God. He has created you in His image to be a worker, giving you skills and abilities to accomplish His purposes. He has also sovereignly placed you in your occupation to do His work there. Even if your job is as lowly as a Roman slave's, it still has value and dignity to Christ.*

Christ is your Boss, but He uses human supervisors. *According to Colossians 3, people in authority over you are*

continued

continued

actually human representatives of Christ. They may not act very Christlike. But in working for them, you are ultimately working for Christ. Do you follow their instructions? Do you shirk your job when they're not around? Are you more interested in impressing them to gain approval and advancement than in getting the job done? How would your work ethic change if you saw Christ as your supervisor?

Christ asks you to put your heart into your work. If you serve Christ in your job, you have more rea-son than anyone else to work with integrity and enthusiasm. The job itself may be unchallenging or unpleasant. But Christ asks you to do it with dignity, to the best of your ability, as though working for Christ Himself.

Christ will reward you for good, faithful work. This passage says that Christ will review your work someday. You can expect praise and reward for working in a Christlike manner. ◆

 Colossians 3:22–24

²²Bondservants, obey in all things your masters according to the flesh, not with eyeservice, as men-pleasers, but in sincerity of heart, fearing God. ²³And whatever you do, do it heartily, as to the Lord and not to men, ²⁴knowing that from the Lord you will receive the reward of the inheritance; for you serve the Lord Christ.

Your Boss

1. Which character most reminds you of your boss? (If you do not have one, think of someone you deal with regularly.)

_____ Superman (or Wonder Woman)
_____ Napoleon
_____ Elmer Fudd
_____ James Dean
_____ Murphy Brown
_____ Lou Grant
_____ Barney the Dinosaur
_____ Jessica Fletcher
_____ Roseanne
_____ Scrooge
_____ Elvis

2. If you had a "wish list," what three things would you change about your boss?

_____

_____

_____

_____

3. Below are some practical ways you can support your boss. On a scale of one to ten, rate how well you have supported your boss recently.

_____ I pray for my boss regularly.
_____ I encourage my boss.
_____ I follow my boss' instructions.
_____ I avoid divisive conversations and conduct among my coworkers.

◆ ◆ ◆ ◆ ◆ ◆ ◆ ◆ ◆

For a few moments, allow your imagination to roam into the realm of science fiction. Your boss has been seriously injured in an airplane crash, but don't worry. We can rebuild your boss. To reconstruct your boss, you can choose traits from a variety of great people from the past and present. (For example: I want my boss to have the creative "tinkering" ability of Henry Ford, the compassion of Mother Teresa, the persuasive personality of Winston Churchill, the integrity of Billy Graham, and the motivational skills of Mary Kay Ash.)
Whose personality traits would you choose for your ideal boss?

_____

_____

Of course, everyone knows that you cannot reconstruct your boss in your own image. But take heart, you already have the Perfect Boss! His name is Jesus Christ, and Colossians 3:22–24 reveals that it is really Christ for whom you are working. Let's take another look at Paul's advice to the Colossians.

1. When Paul instructed the readers of this passage to obey their masters (3:22), he was writing out of the context of slavery. Today, what does the principle of obeying your master mean in your workplace? (For instance: I cheerfully follow my supervisor's instructions; I speak respectfully to my boss's face as well as behind his back.)

_____

_____

2a. The Scripture distinguishes between merely doing your work "as men-pleasers," and doing it "in sincerity of heart, fearing God" (3:22). How does this relate to bidding for brownie points?

_____

_____

_____

2b. Thinking about the events that have occurred in your workplace over the past few weeks, have you been more of a people pleaser or a God pleaser? Give yourself a percentage score.

_____ %   People Pleaser
_____ %   God Pleaser

2c. How would you please God instead of people in your workplace? List some specific things you would do differently.

To please God, I would: To please people, I would:

_____

_____

_____

_____

3. Imagine that Jesus is looking over your shoulder, watching you work. What would you do differently? (Remember, you're answering these questions *honestly!*)

_____

_____

_____

4. How does the concept of Christ as your ultimate Boss relate to the practice of taking pride in your work?

_____

_____

_____

_____

◆ Credit Thieves ◆

"And to conclude my report," Rita Rattinger said to the upper-level managers and their staff members seated around the executive conference table, "I am happy to announce that I have succeeded in securing the Hancock account, including their chain of 127 stores located throughout the United States and Canada."

A collective gasp swept

through the room as the managers and staff members registered their surprise. Mr. Owens, the company's president, bounded to his feet and could barely contain himself as he beamed at Rita across the boardroom. "Outstanding work, Rita! Simply outstanding. Congratulations!"

Seated at the far end of the table, Andrea Smith's mouth was wide open, too, but for entirely different reasons.

I can't believe she did that!

Andrea cried silently. *Hancock was my account!*

It was Andrea who had actually done the groundwork to open the new account. In fact, Rita was totally unaware that the Hancock stores might consider changing suppliers before Andrea brought the matter to her attention. Andrea worked tirelessly, doing her homework on Hancock. She chipped away at the multiple levels of secretaries and pencil pushers until she finally broke through the seemingly airtight seal around Hancock's upper-level

management and established a rapport with the company's decision makers.

It was Andrea who had written the proposal and made the presentation to the Hancock bigwigs. All Rita did was sign her initials, authorizing Andrea's work. Andrea didn't really mind this; after all, she felt that she was contributing to a team effort.

But now, there was Rita stealing the credit for Andrea's work right in front of the boss! ◆

✦ ✦ ✦ ✦ ✦ ✦ ✦ ✦ ✦

Paul refers to "the reward of the inheritance" you will receive from Jesus Christ for your faithful service in Colossians 3:24. The good news is that you can expect a heavenly reward from Jesus for performing your earthly work in a Christlike manner. In this life, recognition from your superiors and financial increases are often granted to the worker who does everything "heartily, as to the Lord and not to men" (Col. 3:23).

The bad news is that some of your coworkers may not appreciate your commitment to excellence. They may balk at your conscientious attempts to do honest, quality work. Maybe your attitude and actions are causing them to look bad before their peers or before their boss. Perhaps they don't share your enthusiasm for the job; perhaps they are jealous of your success.

Consequently, if you are not careful, a counterproductive attitude of competition rather than cooperation can develop between you and your peers. When that happens, tensions heighten for everyone involved. Usually, the cause of such needless conflict comes down to a simple question: Who gets the credit for a job well done, or the blame when the job is botched?

WHO GETS THE CREDIT?

Paul pointed out that the work of planting the church at Corinth was a joint venture between himself, Apollos, and the Lord (1 Cor. 3:5–8). Actually, many others were involved as well. But the point was that cooperation, not competition, is what God desires.

Paul was speaking about the start-up of a church, but the principles apply in the workplace as well. An attitude of competition worries about who gets the credit for success, which is really a selfish concern. By contrast, cooperative efforts over time generally result in achievements far greater than what any individual could do in isolation. That's because the skill, insight, and energy in an organization's work force have enormous potential. But that potential will never be realized if everyone's chief objective is to take credit for results.

Who gets the credit where you work? Do you promote cooperation toward mutual goals rather than competition between individual agendas?

1 Corinthians 3:5–8

⁵Who then is Paul, and who *is* Apollos, but ministers through whom you believed, as the Lord gave to each one? ⁶I planted, Apollos watered, but God gave the increase. ⁷So then neither he who plants is anything, nor he who waters, but God who gives the increase. ⁸Now he who plants and he who waters are one, and each one will receive his own reward according to his own labor.

1. If you were Andrea, what would you have done?

_____

_____

_____

2a. Have you ever been victimized by a "credit thief"? How did you feel?

_____

_____

_____

2b. What (if anything) did you do about it?

_____

_____

_____

3. How do you think you would handle a similar situation today?

_____

_____

_____

4. How do you respond when one of your coworkers receives a promotion, raise, or a new position you feel you should have gotten? (For instance: I feel happy for that person, but resentful toward my superiors; I rejoice with my coworker over his or her success.)

_____

_____

_____

Janna's Story

Janna had just taken a new position at work. She immediately encountered opposition from a coworker for no apparent reason. Here is her story and how she handled the situation:

I tried my best to be a friend to Cheryl, but she insisted on putting me down in front of our boss. I'm sure she thought that by putting me down, she was lifting herself up. Sometimes I wondered if maybe she were right. The boss did seem to pay attention to her negative comments.

I continually tried to turn the other cheek to her insults, and continue to do my job well.

We would go to lunch together and have a great time, but back at work she was cruel and critical toward my work. She always tried to prove that anything I did, she could do better.

One day, Cheryl's bad attitude was more than I could bear, so I confronted her. I said, "Cheryl, you have really been unkind to me today. In fact, you have been harsh with me since I came here. Have I done something to offend you? Is there something wrong?"

Cheryl was shocked at first. Then, after a few minutes, she admitted that I wasn't the real reason for her anger. She and her husband were having trouble with their marriage. Her job was all she had to hold on to; it was the only thing that offered her security.

The situation wasn't resolved that day, but it was the beginning of a mutual understanding between Cheryl and me. She became less critical of me, and I became more patient with her. ◆

♦ ♦ ♦ ♦ ♦ ♦ ♦ ♦ ♦

1. What insight do you get from Janna's story concerning the cause of some types of competition in the workplace?

_____

_____

_____

_____

2a. List some reasons why you think the issue of who gets the credit is more important to some people than to others.

_____

_____

_____

_____

_____

2b. Why should the matter of who gets the credit be less important to a Christian?

_____

_____

_____

3a. Many people are fiercely competitive in everything they do. How can competition be healthy in sports, for example, but often destructive in the workplace?

_____

_____

_____

3b. In your workplace, list some specific things you can do to foster an attitude of cooperation rather than competition among your coworkers.

_____

_____

_____

4. What do you regard as the most important mutual goals of your workplace? (For example: What specific goals are you and your coworkers attempting to obtain as a group?)

_____

_____

_____

_____

5a. In 1 Corinthians 3:5–8, Paul downplays the differences between his role in the church and that of his coworker, Apollos. What was most important to Paul?

_____

_____

_____

_____

5b. With that passage in mind, list several of your coworkers and how you can help or encourage them to do their jobs better. (For instance: I could stay a few minutes after work to help Pete learn the new inventory system.)

_____

_____

_____

6. Someone has said, "The toughest position to play in the orchestra is second fiddle." What does that saying mean?

_____

_____

_____

——◆ What's Fair? ◆——

"Humph! If Bill Roberts is a Christian, I don't want to be one," Charlie said to his friend, Jack.

"Why?" Jack responded, obviously surprised.

"I used to work for him," Charlie replied, "and he was the biggest cheapskate I've ever seen. The company was extremely profitable, but Bill insisted on paying his employees rock-bottom wages. He treated his workers like dirt, unless, of course, you were one of his pets. Bill played favorites constantly. Promotions weren't granted on the basis of work performance, they were based on whether you were one of Bill's buddies.

"He was a liar and a cheat, too. He was always trying to pay somebody 'under the table,' so he wouldn't have to shell out the payroll taxes. Bill can talk about Jesus all he wants, but the Jesus I read about in the Bible wouldn't treat His employees like that!" ◆

◆ ◆ ◆ ◆ ◆ ◆ ◆ ◆ ◆

Labor and management. They coexist like a cat and a dog eyeing each other warily from across the room. The owners want everybody to get along, and for the most part they do. But every once in a while somebody rubs somebody else the wrong way, and the fur begins to fly.

Must labor and management harbor a mutual suspicion of one another? Does the prevailing attitude in the workplace have to be an "us versus them" situation? The New Testament doesn't give that impression at all. Scripture clearly teaches that the proper relationship between labor and management is one of mutual responsibility and respect.

That sounds great, but what does it mean? Don't you wish somebody would spell out the terms of what the labor and management relationship should look like? Somebody has! In fact, God inspired a bunch of somebodies to state His work-world codes so specifically you can't miss them! (You might even want to post these on your desk or on a bulletin board as a reminder.)

WORK-WORLD CODES

Paul's letters have much to say to believers as we live out our faith in the work world. As he does here in Colossians 3:22—4:1, Paul usually speaks to both leaders and workers about the tough character and choices required to honor Christ in a difficult workplace environment. For example:

Guidelines for Managers and Others in Authority

Finance
- Workers deserve payment for their work (1 Cor. 9:7–14).
- You are accountable for fair employee compensation (Col. 4:1).
- Handle wealth very delicately (1Tim. 6:9–10, 17–18).

Work Relationships
- Bring your walk with Christ into each business relationship (2 Cor. 7:1).
- Value people highly (Gal. 5:14–15; Eph. 4:31–32).
- Treat and motivate employees with respect rather than threats (Eph. 6:5–9).
- Have a reasonable view of yourself (Rom. 12:3).

Communication
- Accusations must be verified (Matt. 18:15–35; 2 Cor. 13:1; 1 Tim. 5:19).
- Communication should always be gracious and truthful (Col. 4:6).

Responsibility
- Fulfill your commitments (Rom. 13:6–8).
- Remember your accountability (1 Cor. 3:9–15).
- Care for the poor and the weak (Rom. 12:13; Gal. 2:10).
- Learn how to handle times of bounty and leanness (Phil. 4:12).
- Remember, God's Son gets the ultimate credit (Col. 1:17–18).
- Be sure to care for your own family (1 Tim. 5:8).
- Discern needs and meet them (Titus 3:14).

Management
- View time not only in terms of time management, but also in light of the long-term implications of your decisions (2 Cor. 4:16–18; 2 Pet. 3:8–13).
- Help each employee discern the best thing to do (1 Thess. 5:14–15).
- Be willing to change your opinions (2 Cor. 5:16–17; Philem. 10–14).

Guidelines for Workers and Those under Authority

Tasks
- Don't try to get out of your current situation too quickly (1 Cor. 7:17–24).
- View stress and trouble in perspective (2 Cor. 4:7–18).

Supervisors
- Develop a respect for authority (Rom. 13:1–8).
- Do your work wholeheartedly and respectfully (Eph. 6:5–8; 1 Thess. 5:12–15).
- Give your employers obedient, hard work (Col. 3:22–25; 1 Thess. 4:11–12).
- Honor bosses, whether they are believers or not (1 Tim. 6:1–2).

Coworkers
- Develop a reasonable self-estimate (Rom. 12:3).
- Acknowledge differences and accept the contributions of others (1 Cor. 12:1–8).
- Help others, but do your job (Gal. 6:1–5).
- Learn to speak appropriately and sensitively (Col. 4:6).
- Understand others and treat them respectfully (1 Tim. 5:1–3).
- Develop a reputation for good relationships (Titus 3:1–2).

Responsibility
- Give your whole self to God (Rom. 12:1).
- Develop the art of discernment in order to live responsibly (Eph. 5:15–18).
- Do your work as if working for God—you are (1 Cor. 3:13; Col. 3:17).
- Don't let your responsibilities weigh you down with worry (Phil. 4:6).
- Take responsibility for yourself (1 Thess. 4:11–12; 2 Thess. 3:8–9).
- Develop a godly "workstyle" (Titus 2:9–10).

Finances
- Live frugally and do not steal—including pilfering (Eph. 4:28).
- Care for your family (1Tim. 5:8).

Colossians 3:22— 4:1

22Bondservants, obey in all things your masters according to the flesh, not with eyeservice, as men-pleasers, but in sincerity of heart, fearing God. 23And whatever you do, do it heartily, as to the Lord and not to men, 24knowing that from the Lord you will receive the reward of the inheritance; for you serve the Lord Christ. 25But he who does wrong will be repaid for what he has done, and there is no partiality.

CHAPTER 4

1Masters, give your bondservants what is just and fair, knowing that you also have a Master in heaven.

1. How could the apostle Paul's instructions in Colossians 4:1 have helped Bill Roberts to avoid alienating employees such as Charlie?

_____

_____

_____

2. It is often said, "Good supervision is the act of getting average people to do superior work." How accurately does that statement reflect the attitudes of management and labor in your workplace?

_____ Right on target
_____ Somewhat true
_____ You've got to be kidding

3. How would you respond to someone who suggested to you that good, Christian business ethics make for a bad bottom line?

_____

_____

_____

4a. Based upon the information you have gathered from Colossians 3:22–4:1, finish the following statements:

Employees should _____

_____

_____

Employers should _____

_____

_____

_____

_____

4b. In this passage, Paul provides several motivations for maintaining mutual responsibility and respect between labor and management. Which ones do you regard as most important and why?

_____

_____

_____

_____

_____

———◆ What's Wrong with This Picture? ◆———

Dad came home from a
   hard day's work;
Mom was all up in the air.
Teacher caught Johnny
   stealing some pens
from the grade school called
   Bel-Aire.
Dad turned Johnny over his
   knee,
and Johnny began to
   sob.
Dad said, "Johnny don't
   steal those pens.
I'll bring some home from
   the job!"

◆ ◆ ◆ ◆ ◆ ◆ ◆ ◆ ◆ ◆

Inconsistencies like this one will trip us up every time. And nowhere is this more apparent than in the workplace. Usually it's not the "big sins" that destroy the believer's integrity. More often it is something small and seemingly insignificant—something similar to bringing pens home from the job—that creates the contradictions in the minds of our families, friends, and coworkers regarding the validity of our Christian faith and lifestyle.

For example, you compromise your testimony and cheat your employer (not to mention your coworkers and customers) every time you use company equipment for personal use without permission. Everybody else does it, or, This company owes it to me, you think as you use the company telephones, copy machines, computers, or company car for personal business. And what about calling in sick when you are not? Or your late arrivals and long lunches? Or the "creative" way you tally your expense accounts? In short, how does your workstyle honor Christ? ◆

YOUR "WORKSTYLE"

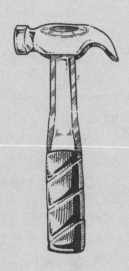

The term "lifestyle" describes the attitudes, behaviors, and expectations you have toward the life you lead. Similarly, the attitudes, behaviors, and expectations you have about your work could be termed your "workstyle." Paul highlights five key areas of a Christlike workstyle in Titus 2:9–10. How does yours compare? (See table.)

According to verse 10, there's a purpose behind this godly workstyle: "that [workers] may adorn the doctrine of God our Savior in all things." Your attitudes and actions on the job can make the gospel of Christ attractive to coworkers and customers. What impression are you making? ◆

FIVE "WORKSTYLE" CATEGORIES

Description	Issue	Application
"obedient to their own masters"	Authority	Do you... •follow instructions? •comply with industry standards? •pay your fair share of taxes?
"well pleasing in all things"	Excellence	Do you... •take pride in your work? •use the right tools for the job, in the right way? •work just as hard even when the boss isn't around?
"not answering back"	Conflict	Do you... •seek to resolve conflicts in a healthy way? •respond with honesty and courtesy? •promote constructive cooperation instead of destructive competition?
"not pilfering"	Honesty & Integrity	Do you... •keep an honest accounting of your hours? •pay for personal expenses rather than charge them to company expense accounts? •avoid making personal long-distance calls on the company's phone?
"showing all good fidelity"	Loyalty & Dependability	Do you... •keep your word? •do what it takes to meet deadlines? •honor what your company stands for?

Titus 2:9–10

⁹*Exhort* bondservants to be obedient to their own masters, to be well pleasing in all *things*, not answering back, ¹⁰not pilfering, but showing all good fidelity, that they may adorn the doctrine of God our Savior in all things.

1. In order of importance, rate those whom you feel you must please by your workstyle.

_____ Mom or Dad
_____ Your spouse
_____ Immediate superiors (foreman, boss, office manager)
_____ Owner of the company or chief executive officer
_____ God
_____ Stockholders
_____ Bill collectors
_____ The Internal Revenue Service
_____ Yourself
_____ Coworkers

2. Check how the following apply to your attitude at work:

Often	Sometimes	Rarely	Never	
____	____	____	____	I disengage myself from "real life" when I enter the workplace.
____	____	____	____	I use my hands (physical strength) but not my head (intelligence).
____	____	____	____	I am more preoccupied with impressing my good-looking coworker than I am in doing quality work.
____	____	____	____	My body is at work, but my brain is elsewhere.
____	____	____	____	I give constructive suggestions to my employer.
____	____	____	____	I accept constructive criticism from my boss.
____	____	____	____	I ease up when the boss isn't watching.
____	____	____	____	I regard my work as an act of honoring God.
____	____	____	____	I follow the rules of my workplace unless they violate God's principles or my own conscience.

3. Which statement reflects your attitude toward your work?

_____ I do a fair day's work for a fair wage.
_____ I do the least amount of work possible for the most pay I can get.

◆ ◆ ◆ ◆ ◆ ◆ ◆ ◆ ◆

As a believer in the workplace, you cannot afford to be sloppy in your workstyle. Somebody always pays for sloppy workmanship. Donna, a dental hygienist, is careless in her clean-up duties. Nowadays, her negligence could cost not only her license and that of her employer, but it could also cost a life. A coworker must come along after Donna and do the job correctly. This costs the dentist more money. Who else pays for Donna's ineptitude?

_____

_____

_____

_____

What are some other ways you can "adorn the doctrine of God" (Titus 2:10) in your workplace? (For instance: I will begin to speak positively and respectfully concerning my boss, my coworkers, and my company.)

_____

_____

_____

_____

◆ ◆ ◆ ◆ ◆ ◆ ◆ ◆ ◆

    The apostle Paul was a realist. In a world divided into masters and slaves, he recognized that somebody was going to be giving orders, and somebody would be taking them. Consequently, Paul instructs us to have a mutual respect for one another. You may be a boss in authority or a worker under authority. Frequently, you are both. In any case, employees and employers are ultimately under the authority of Christ. We must always remember it is Jesus whom we serve, and it is to Him we will one day be accountable.

    In the meantime, how you use the position and the opportunities God has given you will impact your witness for Christ in the workplace. That is the exciting and challenging topic we will explore in our next chapter.

MORE THAN WORDS

You've seen them. You've heard them. They are Christians who give Jesus a bad name in your workplace. They don't walk their talk. They show up late for work and while they are in the workplace, they do inferior work. By their actions and attitudes, they bring the name of Christ into disrepute.

Granted, this group is a minority. Believers with a Christlike workstyle are some of the most productive people in the workplace. But that small segment of complacent, compromising Christians causes such a negative reaction, many employers—even those who are believers—have developed an invisible, but nearly palpable, shield against hiring Christians.

See if you can identify with the employer's sentiments in the following story.

"I WON'T HIRE CHRISTIANS!"

He stood beside a window overlooking the shop floor below. A din of table saws, routers, and other equipment filtered up to the tiny cubicle. His desk was lost under mountains of papers, folders, catalogues, manuals, bills, and an ancient rotary phone.

Turning from the window he sighed and said, "I don't usually hire people who tell me they're Christians. I know that sounds mean. And I don't advertise it. I'm a Christian myself and I try to run this company the way I think God wants it run. But I won't hire Christians!"

"Why not?" he was asked.

"I've been burned once too often," he replied. "I've hired people just because they said they were Christians, and they turned out to be some of the worst employees I ever had.

"I remember one guy was always standing around preaching to the other guys instead of getting his work done. I couldn't afford him! Another guy kept coming in late, day after day. His supervisor warned him. Finally he fired him. Then the fellow came to me to try and get his job back. I told him the supervisor had made the right decision. Know what he said? 'I thought you were a Christian!' Imagine that! He thought he could take advantage of me just because he knew I was a Christian!

"After that I decided: no more Christians!" ◆

1 Timothy 6:1–2

¹Let as many bondservants as are under the yoke count their own masters worthy of all honor, so that the name of God and *His* doctrine may not be blasphemed. ²And those who have believing masters, let them not despise *them* because they are brethren, but rather serve *them* because those who are benefited are believers and beloved. Teach and exhort these things.

"Discrimination!" you may be crying. Yes, it probably is. But you would be hard-pressed to prove it in a court of law; and for the most part, it is preventable discrimination. Christians should have the best reputation in the workplace, not the worst.

♦ ♦ ♦ ♦ ♦ ♦ ♦ ♦ ♦

1a. In your experience, what are some things you have seen or heard that would lend support to the employer's statement, "I won't hire Christians!"?

_____

_____

_____

_____

1b. What experiences have you had that might contradict or disprove the employer's bias?

_____

_____

_____

2a. Employers often have mixed feelings about hiring Christians. Here are some frequently heard reasons for their reluctance to employ believers. Do you agree or disagree with their sentiments? Mark "A" (Agree) or "D" (Disagree) for each statement.

_____ Many Christians in the workplace are unmotivated.
_____ Many Christians feel that since they are employed by another Christian, they shouldn't have to work so hard.
_____ They are selfish.
_____ They have minimal ethics.
_____ They are antagonistic toward others in the workplace.
_____ They spend more time trying to convert their coworkers than they do completing their work.
_____ They seem to have no sense of time; they're rarely punctual.
_____ They tend to form cliques and isolate themselves from the other workers.

2b. What an awful indictment! Ironically, if these complaints concerning Christians in the workplace were reversed, they would present a picture of an extremely desirable employee. Choose four of the statements and turn them around as a positive declaration of your personal workstyle. (For instance, I will be unselfish toward my employer and my coworkers.)

_____

_____

_____

_____

3. Look again at 1 Timothy 6:1–2. According to this passage, why is the idea of a Christian's cheating or manipulating an employer so unacceptable?

_____

_____

_____

4. In verse 2, the apostle Paul cautions believers not to despise (or show disrespect) to their believing masters. What are some ways a Christian may be guilty of disrespecting a boss? (For instance: I call my boss by her first name when everyone else refers to her as Mrs. Smith.)

_____

_____

_____

_____

◆ Your Witness versus Your Work ◆

"Come on, Carl!" Brian implored. "We better hurry. Everyone else is back from lunch except you and me. And you know what Mr. Hamilton said last week at the staff meeting about being on time. Do you think he'd really fire anybody for being late?"

"Oh, don't worry about old Ham-bones. He talks big, but that's all it is; just talk. Anyhow, what you and I are discussing is important. We're talking about eternity! Where is your soul going to spend forever?"

"Well, I'm interested in what you have to say about Jesus and all that Bible stuff, but right now I have to get back to work. Mr. Hamilton wants those cost projections done today." Brian hurried to his work station and began busying himself with the stack of papers he had left unfinished when Carl had come by to go to lunch—fifteen minutes early.

"Okay, okay," Carl chuckled, as he ambled toward his desk. "I'll catch you later. Don't work too hard."

Twenty minutes later, Carl was back at Brian's work station. He was carrying a Bible in one hand and a cup of coffee in the other. "You know, I've been thinking," he said as he leaned his shoulder against Brian's doorway. "The Bible says 'today is the day of salvation,' so you better repent right now. Who knows, you might drop dead before you get home tonight. Then where would you be?"

Brian stopped crunching numbers long enough to look at Carl. He gritted his teeth and said slowly, "Carl, if I don't get this work done, I may as well be dead!"

"Just my point," Carl continued, "the Bible says that it is appointed unto man once to die and then he faces the judgment . . ."

"Ah-hem!" a loud voice interrupted their conversation. "And just what does the Bible say about unemployment?"

"Mr. Hamilton!" Brian and Carl said simultaneously. ◆

◆ ◆ ◆ ◆ ◆ ◆ ◆ ◆ ◆

To witness for Christ is to offer a true representation of Christ, your personal experience of Christ, and His good news for all people. This may involve words or deeds or both. Yet many Christians are reluctant to say anything about their faith in Christ, especially in the workplace. On the other hand, some believers see the workplace as an ideal platform for evangelism since they have a "captive audience." What do you think is the best approach? Check the statements that apply to you.

_____ I greet every new acquaintance with, "Hi! I'm Willie Witness and if you'd like to become a Christian, you can find me at . . ."

_____ My faith is personal and private. I keep it to myself. Religious talk belongs at home and in church, not in the workplace.

_____ I look at my coworkers as lost sheep in need of a Shepherd.

_____ Religion and politics are two topics I don't discuss at work.

_____ If someone asks me about my faith, I'm always glad to share it with them. But I don't usually initiate conversations about Jesus.

So what's a believer to do? You want to share the good news about Christ, but you don't want to offend your coworkers. You want to please your Lord, but you also want to please your employer. To help you establish a balance between your witness and your work, take a look at the article "Work—A Platform for Evangelism."

WORK—A PLATFORM FOR EVANGELISM?

Our jobs put us in touch with people like no other activity. For 40 or more hours a week we toil, laugh, struggle, and interact with others to accomplish tasks. For that reason, many Christians view their workplace as a primary platform for spreading the gospel. Is that legitimate?

It is certainly legitimate to treat our workplace as an opportunity for unbelievers to see Christianity by looking at us. Indeed, Paul challenges us to display a godly workstyle for that reason (Titus 2:9–10). However, we must never emphasize verbal witness to the detriment of our work, as if God sends us into the work world *only* to use it as a platform for evangelism.

Employers rightly look down on workers who are intruders, deceivers, or sluggards. In Ephesians 6:5–9, Paul challenges us to work with "sincerity of heart" and to pay close attention to the work itself, which he calls "doing the will of God." That's what impresses one's employer, as well as God.

Ephesians 6:5–9

[5]Bondservants, be obedient to those who are your masters according to the flesh, with fear and trembling, in sincerity of heart, as to Christ; [6]not with eyeservice, as men-pleasers, but as bondservants of Christ, doing the will of God from the heart, [7]with goodwill doing service, as to the Lord, and not to men, [8]knowing that whatever good anyone does, he will receive the same from the Lord, whether *he is* a slave or free.

[9]And you, masters, do the same things to them, giving up threatening, knowing that your own Master also is in heaven, and there is no partiality with Him.

1a. Have you ever had anyone witness to you at your workplace?

_____ No   _____ Yes

1b. If you answered *no,* how does that make you feel? (Circle one.)

Ignored   Nobody cares   Perfectly fine   Comfortable   Happy

1c. If you answered *yes,* how does that make you feel? (Circle one).

Special   Happy   Okay   Angry   Confused

2. How did that person approach you concerning your relationship to Jesus? How did he or she bring up the subject?

_____

_____

_____

_____

3. What about that person's personality or message attracted you to (or distracted you from) Jesus?

_____

_____

_____

_____

_____

Employers Have Rights, Too!

In Ephesians 6:5–9, the apostle Paul encourages responsibility and integrity between slaves and masters. In Paul's day, slaves played an important role in the work world. When many slaves and their owners became Christians, their relationship to each other was no longer simply servant and master; they became brothers and sisters in Christ. What were they to do now? How were they to function in their society? Although Paul did not overtly condemn or condone slavery, he did give them some good rules to live by. The principles apply to our relationships between employees and employers in today's workplace, too.

♦ ♦ ♦ ♦ ♦ ♦ ♦ ♦ ♦

1. According to Ephesians 6:5–9, what do you owe your employer or employees?

_____

_____

_____

_____

_____

2. How do you think that should affect your witness at work?

_____

_____

_____

_____

_____

3. Ephesians 6:6 implies that by applying yourself in the workplace you are "doing the will of God." List some specific ways you can do God's will in your workplace.

_____

_____

_____

_____

——◆ Talk Is Cheap ◆——

Valerie wanted to introduce Chrissie to the Lord, but Chrissie refused to respond to Valerie's efforts. The two women rode to work together, and every day Valerie attempted to plant a "gospel seed" in Chrissie's heart. Every chance she got, Valerie talked to her coworker about Christianity. She lectured Chrissie about her immoral lifestyle and criticized the way she dressed for work. Chrissie didn't argue with Valerie, nor did she antagonize Valerie; she simply didn't care.

Finally, Valerie decided that she would quit lecturing Chrissie and start loving her. "I realized," said Valerie, "that my motives for witnessing to Chrissie were wrong. I wasn't doing it for Jesus or for Chrissie; I was doing it for me! I began praying for Chrissie every day, and I never told her what I was doing.

"I stopped nagging her about her lifestyle and her clothes. I've made a promise to myself that if I can't say something to Chrissie in a loving way, I won't say it at all. And then, on the way to work yesterday she asked me what it means to be forgiven. Through it all, I've learned that I have to earn the right to be heard." ◆

◆ ◆ ◆ ◆ ◆ ◆ ◆ ◆ ◆

How about you? Have you earned the right to be heard in your workplace? Perhaps your coworkers are saying, "Talk is cheap; let's see you live it. We don't necessarily need more information about the Christian life. We want to see the real thing lived out in front of us."

And they are correct. To earn the right to be heard, we need to present evidence before information.

EVIDENCE BEFORE INFORMATION

What evidence can new believers offer to validate their new faith? How can their commitment to Christ be seen as more than just one more spiritual path among many? They need to put their best foot forward among nonbelievers, spiritually speaking, but how?

Believers on the island of Crete faced such a challenge, and it was enormous. The Cretan culture had many gods. Its people filled their time with much idle chatter, empty promises, and lies (Titus 1:10–13). So how could the Christians' loyalty to yet one more God be taken seriously, let alone make any difference in the society?

Paul acknowledged the dilemma that these early believers faced by opening his letter to Titus with the affirmation that God never lies (1:2). In the same way, God's people must be people of truth and unimpeachable integrity. How can that happen? Through fewer words and more deeds. That was the way to build consistent evidence of a new and credible lifestyle with lasting impact.

continued

continued

The apostle called for that strategy among several sub-groups of the new believers: older men (2:2), older women (2:3), younger women (2:4–5), younger men (2:6), Titus himself (2:7–8), and slaves (2:9–10). Each of these groups was to carry out the deeds of faith listed in 3:1–8. In fact, Paul insisted that they all "be careful to maintain good works" (v. 8). They were to avoid extended arguments as unprofitable and useless in their witness.

Do your coworkers see the Christlike deeds of believers where you work? Or has their main exposure to the faith been little more than Christians filling the air with statements and ideas? Has your own walk with Christ produced any visible fruit in front of your associates, such as patience, staying power, compassion, loyalty, better management, hard work, or faithful service? That's the kind of evidence that shows whether faith in Christ has any power and impact. ◆

Titus 3:1–8

¹Remind them to be subject to rulers and authorities, to obey, to be ready for every good work, ²to speak evil of no one, to be peaceable, gentle, showing all humility to all men. ³For we ourselves were also once foolish, disobedient, deceived, serving various lusts and pleasures, living in malice and envy, hateful and hating one another. ⁴But when the kindness and the love of God our Savior toward man appeared, ⁵not by works of righteousness which we have done, but according to His mercy He saved us, through the washing of regeneration and renewing of the Holy Spirit, ⁶whom He poured out on us abundantly through Jesus Christ our Savior, ⁷that having been justified by His grace we should become heirs according to the hope of eternal life.

⁸This is a faithful saying, and these things I want you to affirm constantly, that those who have believed in God should be careful to maintain good works. These things are good and profitable to men.

Paul wrote the letter known as Titus *to one of his coworkers who was pastoring the church Paul had founded on the island of Crete. The Cretans worshiped many false gods, including numerous idols of their own making. In the midst of this corrupt culture, Paul encouraged Titus to urge the believers to model authentic Christianity.*

1a. List some idols and false gods our contemporary culture is worshiping. (For instance, power, money, prestige.)

_____

_____

_____

_____

_____

1b. How can you model authentic Christianity in regard to each of the false gods you listed in 1a? (For instance: I will acknowledge that God is the owner of my material possessions; as a token reminder of that, I will give a minimum of ten percent of my income to God's work.)

_____

_____

_____

_____

2. In Titus 3:1–2, Paul lists seven practical things believers can do to model the Christian life in our communities. List these things and describe briefly how you can practice each principle in your workplace. Be as specific as possible.

_____

_____

_____

_____

_____

3. In verse 3, Paul describes what he and the Cretans used to be like before they trusted Jesus. Check the phrases that describe your life before you trusted Christ.

_____ Foolish (concerning the things of God)
_____ Disobedient (to the Word of God and the will of God)
_____ Deceived (possibly by other people, philosophies, or by the devious devices of the devil)
_____ Serving various lusts and pleasures
_____ Living in malice and envy

4. Next, in verses 4–7, Paul summarizes what Jesus does for us when He saves us. Scan the verses and jot down Paul's points that seem to stand out for you.

_____

_____

_____

_____

_____

5. When you combine verse 3 with verses 4–7 you can easily see a pattern for your personal testimony: "I once was _____, but since trusting Jesus as my Savior, He has done _____ in my life, and I now am _____."

Write a brief description of your personal testimony in the space below.

I once was _____

_____

_____

_____

Since I have trusted Jesus, _____

_____

_____

_____

_____

◆ ◆ ◆ ◆ ◆ ◆ ◆ ◆ ◆

As you model authentic Christianity in your workplace, opportunities will open for you to present your personal testimony. There's something wonderfully attractive about Christianity; it's contagious! Your coworkers will want to know more about who Jesus is, what He means to you, what He has done in your life, and, quite possibly, how they can come to know Him! Your personal testimony, demonstrated in a workstyle that has earned you the right to be heard, might have a world-changing impact.

◆ The Power of a Personal Testimony ◆

It's a familiar story, but is one that bears repeating. A simple Sunday school teacher named Kimbell introduced a shoe clerk to Jesus. The shoe clerk was Dwight L. Moody.

Moody became one of America's greatest evangelists. Thousands of people met Jesus through his preaching, and the ministry that bears his name still flourishes and reaches out to the world from downtown Chicago. One young preacher upon whom Moody's ministry had a profound influence was Frederick B. Meyer.

F. B. Meyer became one of the most beloved preachers of his day. Besides a busy preaching schedule, he served as president of the World Baptist Alliance. His ministry had a tremendous impact during his lifetime, and his books continue to bless, challenge, and encourage Christians today.

F. B. Meyer preached frequently on college campuses. On one campus, a young man named J. Wilbur Chapman came to know Christ. Following his conversion, Chapman involved himself in the YMCA, where he arranged for a former professional baseball player named Billy Sunday to come to Charlotte, North Carolina for a series of "revival" services. The services were extremely suc-cessful and many people com-mitted their lives to Christ. As a result of Sunday's efforts, a group of Charlotte civic lead-ers invited another evangelist, Mordecai Hamm to conduct revival services at a later date. Under Hamm's preaching, an-other young man surrendered his life to Jesus Christ. You may not be familiar with the other names in this story, but you know this man's name: Billy Graham. ◆

✦ ✦ ✦ ✦ ✦ ✦ ✦ ✦ ✦

Consider this: When that Sunday school teacher first shared the gospel with that young shoe clerk back in the 1800's, he probably never dreamed his words and actions would be the indirect cause of literally millions and millions of people coming to know Jesus Christ. But that's what happened! Today, a myriad of people who have been influenced by Billy Graham's min-istry continue the legacy by sharing the message of Christ with millions more. Never under-estimate the power of your personal testimony!

Of course, every opportunity to witness is as different as the people and circumstances involved. That's nothing new. God has always loved variety. He doesn't force people into rigid religious categories in order to receive the gospel.

Jesus never tried to cram His message down people's throats. Nor did the apostle Paul develop a "gospel spiel" and then travel around the Mediterranean spouting off the same rou-tine. On the contrary, Paul adjusted his approach according to the needs of his listeners. He at-tempted to meet them where they were and present the gospel to them in a way that they would most easily understand and most likely accept. We need to learn how to do the same.

AUDIENCE-SHAPED MESSAGES

*A*s a Christian, do you know how to commu-nicate the message of Christ to the different audiences you encounter? Or do you use the same old formula time after time, no matter who is listening? For that matter, do you remain silent when you have the opportunity to speak up for Christ, because you simply don't know what to say?

Paul had no prepackaged gospel message. He varied his approach with the situation. He was as aware of the differences between his audiences as he was of the content of his faith. Acts records numerous encounters, among them:

(1) Jews in the synagogue at Antioch of Pisidia (Acts 13:14–43).

• Paul reviewed the history of the Jewish faith, summarizing it from the Old Testament (vv. 17–22).

• He told how that history led to Jesus (vv. 23–37).

• He pointed out his audience's need to accept Jesus as their Messiah (vv. 38–41).

• He responded to their re-sistance by clearly explain-ing the alternative (vv. 46–48).

Result:

• Many chose to follow the way of Christ (v. 43).

• Others reacted negatively and opposed Paul (v. 45).

• Troublemakers incited city

continued

continued

leaders to persecute Paul and his companions (v. 50).

(2) Intellectuals at Athens (17:16–33).

- Paul prepared by observing and reflecting on their culture (v. 16).
- He addressed them on their own turf, the Areopagus (vv. 19, 22).
- He established common ground, beginning with what was familiar and meaningful to them (vv. 22–23a, 28).
- He bridged to a description of God as the Creator and sustainer of life, distinguishing Him from the pagan idols that the Athenians worshiped (vv. 23b–29).
- He challenged them to repentance and appealed to the resurrection of Christ as proof that what he was telling them was true (vv. 30–31).

Result:

- Some mocked (v. 32).
- Some wanted to hear more (v. 32).
- Some believed (v. 34–35).

(3) An angry mob in Jerusalem (21:27—22:21).

- Paul built a bridge by reminding them of his own Jewish heritage (21:30).
- He reminded them that he, too, had once detested Jesus' followers; in fact, he had persecuted them (22:4–5).
- He explained the process by which he had changed his mind and joined a movement that he once opposed (vv. 6–17).

Result:

- Already at fever pitch (21:27–30), the crowd erupted violently, demanding Paul's death (22:22–23).

(4) High officials in a Roman court (26:1–32).

- Paul described his religious heritage (vv. 4–5).
- He related his view of his opponents' charges against him (vv. 6–8).
- He recalled his previous opposition to Jesus' followers (vv. 9–11).

- He recounted his own life-changing encounter with Christ (vv. 12–19).
- He explained the fundamentals of Jesus' message and the implications for his non-Jewish listeners (vv. 20–23).

Result:

- The rulers listened carefully (vv. 24, 31–32).
- They challenged his application of the gospel to them (vv. 24, 28).
- They passed him on in the Roman judicial process, thereby foiling a Jewish plot against him (vv. 31–32).

The gospel itself is forever the same, but as Christ's followers we are called to shape our message to fit our various audiences. How do your coworkers and friends differ from each other? What effect should that have on your life and message for them? What aspects of the good news would they most likely respond to? Do you know how they view faith? Why not ask them—before you speak? ◆

 Acts 26:1–32

¹Then Agrippa said to Paul, "You are permitted to speak for yourself."

So Paul stretched out his hand and answered for himself: ²"I think myself happy, King Agrippa, because today I shall answer for myself before you concerning all the things of which I am accused by the Jews, ³especially because you are expert in all customs and questions which have to do with the Jews. Therefore I beg you to hear me patiently.

⁴"My manner of life from my youth, which was spent from the beginning among my own nation at Jerusalem, all the Jews know. ⁵They knew me from the first, if they were willing to testify, that according to the strictest sect of our religion I lived a Pharisee. ⁶And now I stand and am judged for the hope of the promise made by God to our fathers. ⁷To this *promise* our twelve tribes,

continued

continued

earnestly serving *God* night and day, hope to attain. For this hope's sake, King Agrippa, I am accused by the Jews. ⁸Why should it be thought incredible by you that God raises the dead?

⁹"Indeed, I myself thought I must do many things contrary to the name of Jesus of Nazareth. ¹⁰This I also did in Jerusalem, and many of the saints I shut up in prison, having received authority from the chief priests; and when they were put to death, I cast my vote against *them.* ¹¹And I punished them often in every synagogue and compelled *them* to blaspheme; and being exceedingly enraged against them, I persecuted *them* even to foreign cities.

¹²"While thus occupied, as I journeyed to Damascus with authority and commission from the chief priests, ¹³at midday, O king, along the road I saw a light from heaven, brighter than the sun, shining around me and those who journeyed with me. ¹⁴And when we all had fallen to the ground, I heard a voice speaking to me and saying in the Hebrew language, 'Saul, Saul, why are you persecuting Me? *It is* hard for you to kick against the goads.' ¹⁵So I said, 'Who are You, Lord?' And He said, 'I am Jesus, whom you are persecuting. ¹⁶But rise and stand on your feet; for I have appeared to you for this purpose, to make you a minister and a witness both of the things which you have seen and of the things which I will yet reveal to you. ¹⁷I will deliver you from the *Jewish* people, as well as *from* the Gentiles, to whom I now send you, ¹⁸to open their eyes, *in order* to turn *them* from darkness to light, and *from* the power of Satan to God, that they may receive forgiveness of sins and an inheritance among those who are sanctified by faith in Me.'

¹⁹"Therefore, King Agrippa, I was not disobedient to the heavenly vision, ²⁰but declared first to those in Damascus and in Jerusalem, and throughout all the region of Judea, and *then* to the Gentiles, that they should repent, turn to God, and do works befitting repentance. ²¹For these reasons the Jews seized me in the temple and tried to kill *me.* ²²Therefore, having obtained help from God, to this day I stand, witnessing both to small and great, saying no other things than those which the prophets and Moses said would come— ²³that the Christ would suffer, that He would be the first to rise from the dead, and would proclaim light to the *Jewish* people and to the Gentiles."

²⁴Now as he thus made his defense, Festus said with a loud voice, "Paul, you are beside yourself! Much learning is driving you mad!"

²⁵But he said, "I am not mad, most noble Festus, but speak the words of truth and reason. ²⁶For the king, before whom I also speak freely, knows these things; for I am convinced that none of these things escapes his attention, since this thing was not done in a corner. ²⁷King Agrippa, do you believe the prophets? I know that you do believe."

²⁸Then Agrippa said to Paul, "You almost persuade me to become a Christian."

²⁹And Paul said, "I would to God that not only you, but also all who hear me today, might become both almost and altogether such as I am, except for these chains."

³⁰When he had said these things, the king stood up, as well as the governor and Bernice and those who sat with them; ³¹and when they had gone aside, they talked among themselves, saying, "This man is doing nothing deserving of death or chains."

³²Then Agrippa said to Festus, "This man might have been set free if he had not appealed to Caesar."

With all due respect to evangelistic crusades, Christian radio and television programs, Christian concerts, books, and tapes, the best method of sharing the gospel with people is still one-on-one. That's why your witness in your workplace may be more important than anything else when it comes to your coworkers' meeting Christ.

Unquestionably, the best opportunities for personal evangelism exist where you have had the time to build a solid relationship. That person working right next to you, for example, or the security guard you greet every day as you go in or out of your workplace—these are prime opportunities for you to present a positive message about Jesus. Who knows? Maybe God has placed these people in your path for that specific purpose.

On the other hand, many witnessing opportunities seem to just pop up unexpectedly. For example, the conversation in the lunch room suddenly takes a spiritual turn. You need to know the gospel message and how to present it in a palatable form.

◆ ◆ ◆ ◆ ◆ ◆ ◆ ◆ ◆

1a. How would you answer if one of your coworkers asked you, "What is the gospel?"

_____

_____

_____

_____

1b. What did the apostle Paul choose to emphasize in his presentation in Acts 26:20–23?

_____

_____

2. How did Paul seek to build bridges into the lives of his listeners in each of the accounts noted in the article, "Audience-Shaped Messages"?

_____

_____

_____

_____

3. Think of two friends or acquaintances in your workplace. What approach do you think would be most effective in communicating the gospel to each of them? Write down your friends' names and the best approach you could use to tell them about Jesus.

Name: _____

The approach I would use: _____

_____

_____

Name: _____

The approach I would use: _____

_____

_____

_____

——◆ Everybody Ought to Know ◆——

"I'm nervous about telling my coworkers about Jesus," Donna admitted. "Maybe I lack confidence in my own ability to present the message, or maybe I'm uncertain whether the gospel will work for them. Frankly, I'm afraid my coworkers will make fun of me or get angry at me for talking to them about Jesus. Do you really think they want to know?"

Yes, they do! But don't worry if you do not know exactly how to tell people about Jesus. You have a very effective way to communicate Christ's message—show it to them.

Every day, in everything you do, you spread the gospel simply by adopting attitudes that reflect Jesus' love and compassion for others. When you show genuine concern for your coworkers, you show them Christ. When you do your work honestly and fairly, you reflect Jesus' message. When you turn down a shady business deal, you spread the gospel.

As you present Christ in your workplace, you don't need to be self-conscious; you can be Christ-conscious. After all, it is His image your coworkers need to see. ◆

IMAGE-CONSCIOUS

When other people look at you, what do they see? What image do you project to coworkers, customers, friends, and neighbors? As Paul traveled through the cities of the Roman Empire, he always gave thought to how he would be perceived, but his biggest concern was whether observers would see Jesus in him.

To illustrate this principle, Paul recalled a phenomenon that occurred during the period in which Moses received the Law. As Israel wandered through the wilderness, God revealed Himself to the people through what looked like a consuming fire (Ex. 24:17). But to Moses He spoke face to face (33:11). This encounter with the Living God had such an effect on Moses that his face would shine with an afterglow whenever he returned to the people. To dispel their fear, he put a veil over his face to hide the glory that resulted from his proximity to God.

Paul argues that we as believers have an even closer proximity to God than Moses did, for God Himself lives inside us (2 Cor. 3:8). Thus, when we meet others, they ought to see the glory of God shining out of us (2 Cor. 3:9–11, 18). In other words, they ought to see Jesus.

Is that who people see when they look at us? Do they see Jesus' love, integrity, and power? Or do we "veil" the Light of the World (Matt. 5:14–16) under a mask of selfish ambition and worldly concerns?

2 Corinthians 3:17–18

[17]Now the Lord is the Spirit; and where the Spirit of the Lord is, there *is* liberty. [18]But we all, with unveiled face, beholding as in a mirror the glory of the Lord, are being transformed into the same image from glory to glory, just as by the Spirit of the Lord.

---

1. Paul emphasizes in 2 Corinthians 3:17–18 that our lives should reflect the glory of the Lord. God is the light, and we reflect His "holy glow" to others after we have spent time in God's presence. How would you describe the light you have been reflecting recently in your workplace?

_____ A candle   _____ A ray of sunshine
_____ A flashlight   _____ A neon sign
_____ A spotlight   _____ A burned out lightbulb

2. Here are some of the ways Jesus built bridges into His listeners' lives as He told them about the gospel. Mark "Y" (Yes) or "N" (No) for the ways you are reflecting His image in your workplace.

_____Jesus made Himself available to people; do you?
_____He observed common courtesy as He presented the gospel; do you?
_____Jesus communicated with people on their own level of understanding; do you?
_____He complimented people when possible; do you?
_____Jesus listened carefully and sincerely to people's stories; do you?
_____Jesus never argued with unbelievers; do you?

◆ ◆ ◆ ◆ ◆ ◆ ◆ ◆ ◆

Is it really possible to be an effective witness for Jesus Christ in your workplace, without losing your job, your friends, or your sanity? Yes, it is! But witnessing is not all talk; it involves doing your work in a Christlike manner, genuinely caring about your coworkers, and presenting a consistent and accurate message of Christ's love.

Are your coworkers really cold and hardhearted, not caring about heaven or hell or abundant life here and now? Or, are we failing to communicate the message in a language and manner they can understand? As a believer, your primary job is not to condemn or criticize your coworkers, nor is it to convert them. Your concern is to help your coworkers see Jesus.

It is not always easy to represent Christ in the workplace, especially when the people with whom you work are so different from you. In the next chapter we're going to discover how you can better deal with people in your workplace who don't view life from the same perspective as you.

DON'T DISCOUNT DIVERSITY

The fear of strangers or a fear of the unknown is a condition that affects all of us at some point in our lives. This condition, known as xenophobia, does not always have a distinctive cause.

Often the reasons for our hatred and fear make little sense; frequently, the cause for the animosity is shrouded in the dense fog of the distant past. And this hatred and fear continue to be passed on from generation to generation.

We don't know when xenophobia began, but we do know it existed in Jesus' day. If ever two groups of people harbored long-standing suspicion, fear, and hatred of each other, they were the Jews and the Samaritans. Here's why.

"JEWS HAVE NO DEALINGS WITH SAMARITANS"

Hatred between Jews and Samaritans was fierce and long-standing. In some ways, it dated all the way back to the days of the patriarchs. Jacob (or Israel) had twelve sons, whose descendants became twelve tribes. Joseph, his favorite, was despised by the other brothers (Gen. 37:3–4), and they attempted to do away with him.

But God intervened and not only preserved Joseph's life, but used him to preserve the lives of the entire clan. Before his death, Jacob gave Joseph a blessing in which he called him a "fruitful bough by a well" (Gen. 49:22). The blessing was fulfilled, as the territory allotted to the tribes of Joseph's two sons, Ephraim ("doubly fruitful") and Manasseh, was the fertile land that eventually became Samaria.

Later, Israel divided into two kingdoms. The northern kingdom, called Israel, established its capital first at Shechem, a revered site in Jewish history, and later at the hilltop city of Samaria.

In 722 B.C. Assyria conquered Israel and took most of its people into captivity. The invaders then brought in Gentile colonists "from Babylon, Cuthah, Ava, Hamath, and from Sepharvaim" (2 Kin. 17:24) to resettle the land. The

continued

continued

foreigners brought with them their pagan idols, which the remaining Jews began to worship alongside the God of Israel (2 Kin. 17:29–41). Intermarriages also took place (Ezra 9:1—10:44; Neh. 13:23–28).

Meanwhile, the southern kingdom of Judah fell to Babylon in 600 B.C. Its people, too, were carried off into captivity. But 70 years later, a remnant of 43,000 was permitted to return and rebuild Jerusalem. The people who now inhabited the former northern kingdom—the Samaritans—vigorously opposed the repatriation and tried to undermine the attempt to reestablish the nation. For their part, the full-blooded, monotheistic Jews detested the mixed marriages and worship of their northern cousins. So walls of bitterness were erected on both sides and did nothing but harden for the next 550 years.

There are countless modern parallels to the Jewish-Samaritan enmity—indeed, wherever peoples are divided by racial and ethnic barriers. Perhaps that's why the Gospels and Acts provide so many instances of Samaritans coming into contact with the message of Jesus. It is not the person from the radically different culture on the other side of the world that is hardest to love, but the nearby neighbor whose skin color, language, rituals, values, ancestry, history, and customs are different from one's own.

Jews had no dealings with the Samaritans. With whom do you have no dealings? ◆

   John 4:4–42

⁴But He needed to go through Samaria.

⁵So He came to a city of Samaria which is called Sychar, near the plot of ground that Jacob gave to his son Joseph. ⁶Now Jacob's well was there. Jesus therefore, being wearied from *His* journey, sat thus by the well. It was about the sixth hour.

⁷A woman of Samaria came to draw water. Jesus said to her, "Give Me a drink." ⁸For His disciples had gone away into the city to buy food.

⁹Then the woman of Samaria said to Him, "How is it that You, being a Jew, ask a drink from me, a Samaritan woman?" For Jews have no dealings with Samaritans.

¹⁰Jesus answered and said to her, "If you knew the gift of God, and who it is who says to you, 'Give Me a drink,' you would have asked Him, and He would have given you living water."

¹¹The woman said to Him, "Sir, You have nothing to draw with, and the well is deep. Where then do You get that living water? ¹²Are You greater than our father Jacob, who gave us the well, and drank from it himself, as well as his sons and his livestock?"

¹³Jesus answered and said to her, "Whoever drinks of this water will thirst again, ¹⁴but whoever drinks of the water that I shall give him will never thirst. But the water that I shall give him will become in him a fountain of water springing up into everlasting life."

¹⁵The woman said to Him, "Sir, give me this water, that I may not thirst, nor come here to draw."

¹⁶Jesus said to her, "Go, call your husband, and come here."

¹⁷The woman answered and said, "I have no husband."

Jesus said to her, "You have well said, 'I have no husband,' ¹⁸for you have had five husbands, and the one whom you now have is not your husband; in that you spoke truly."

¹⁹The woman said to Him, "Sir, I perceive that You are a prophet. ²⁰Our fathers worshiped on this mountain, and you *Jews* say that in Jerusalem is the place where one ought to worship."

²¹Jesus said to her, "Woman, believe Me, the hour is coming when you will neither on this mountain, nor in Jerusalem, worship the Father. ²²You worship what you do not know; we know what we worship, for salvation is of the Jews.

continued

continued

²³But the hour is coming, and now is, when the true worshipers will worship the Father in spirit and truth; for the Father is seeking such to worship Him. ²⁴God *is* Spirit, and those who worship Him must worship in spirit and truth."

²⁵The woman said to Him, "I know that Messiah is coming" (who is called Christ). "When He comes, He will tell us all things."

²⁶Jesus said to her, "I who speak to you am *He.*"

²⁷And at this *point* His disciples came, and they marveled that He talked with a woman; yet no one said, "What do You seek?" or, "Why are You talking with her?"

²⁸The woman then left her waterpot, went her way into the city, and said to the men, ²⁹"Come, see a Man who told me all things that I ever did. Could this be the Christ?" ³⁰Then they went out of the city and came to Him.

³¹In the meantime His disciples urged Him, saying, "Rabbi, eat."

³²But He said to them, "I have food to eat of which you do not know."

³³Therefore the disciples said to one another, "Has anyone brought Him *anything* to eat?"

³⁴Jesus said to them, "My food is to do the will of Him who sent Me, and to finish His work. ³⁵Do you not say, 'There are still four months and *then* comes the harvest'? Behold, I say to you, lift up your eyes and look at the fields, for they are already white for harvest! ³⁶And he who reaps receives wages, and gathers fruit for eternal life, that both he who sows and he who reaps may rejoice together. ³⁷For in this the saying is true: 'One sows and another reaps.' ³⁸I sent you to reap that for which you have not labored; others have labored, and you have entered into their labors."

³⁹And many of the Samaritans of that city believed in Him because of the word of the woman who testified, "He told me all that I *ever* did." ⁴⁰So when the Samaritans had come to Him, they urged Him to stay with them; and He stayed there two days. ⁴¹And many more believed because of His own word.

⁴²Then they said to the woman, "Now we believe, not because of what you said, for we ourselves have heard *Him* and we know that this is indeed the Christ, the Savior of the world."

Almost all of us have experienced prejudice toward a person or group, or we have been on the receiving end of prejudicial treatment from a person or group. Circle an "A" for those groups you have felt prejudice toward, and a "B" for those groups from whom you have received prejudicial treatment. Some groups may require more than one answer.

A	B	Christians	A	B	White collar workers
A	B	Non-Christians	A	B	Blue collar worker
A	B	Blacks	A	B	Republicans
A	B	Whites	A	B	Democrats
A	B	Orientals	A	B	Rich people
A	B	Native Americans	A	B	Poor people
A	B	Cigarette smokers	A	B	Men
A	B	Non-smokers	A	B	Women

Now, giving yourself one point for each A or B, total your score and write the number in the spaces below.

I have felt prejudice toward ＿＿ groups of people.
I have felt prejudice from ＿＿ groups of people.

You can develop a prejudicial attitude about almost anything in life. Some of these are merely silly attitudes, but many of these feelings of enmity toward other people are destructive. If you find yourself holding on to bitterness toward somebody else, now is a good time to turn away from those attitudes and to ask God to forgive you. Only when you are freed from your own chains of racial, ethnic, or cultural bondage are you free to share the love of Christ with those who hold views different from yours.

Jesus Meets and Beats Ethnic Bias

During the time Jesus taught on earth, He was considered to be a rabbi. A strict Jewish rabbi would not speak to a woman in public, not even to members of his own family. Some of the more legalistic Pharisees shut their eyes when they saw a woman walking toward them on the streets. To emphasize their piety, these foolish Pharisees would keep on walking with their eyes closed until they banged into something.

Not only was Jesus' encounter in John 4:4–42 with a woman, but she was also from the region of Samaria. And, as we have already seen, the Jews and the Samaritans held longstanding grudges against each other (4:9). Furthermore, this woman was of questionable moral character. She had been married five times and she was not married to the man with whom she was living when she met Jesus (4:17–18).

The Samaritan woman came to the well at noon (the sixth hour), which was a very hot time of day. Most of the other women of the village drew their water early in the morning or in the evening. So why was this woman at the well at this hour? Was she attempting to avoid the other women in town? Was she hoping to meet another man? We can only guess. Regardless of her reasons for being at the well at this time (maybe she was thirsty!), no respectable rabbi would have wanted to be seen in her company, let alone be seen carrying on a conversation with her! But Jesus refused to let sexual, racial, or ethnic prejudices prevent Him from spreading His message of love, forgiveness, and reconciliation with God.

❖ ❖ ❖ ❖ ❖ ❖ ❖ ❖ ❖

1. What do you think the reaction would be if your pastor were seen talking to a prostitute in a seedy part of town at a time when most "respectable folks" were either working or sleeping?

_____

_____

_____

2. Why do you suppose the disciples did not say anything to the woman or to Jesus, even though they were surprised that He was talking with her (4:27)?

_____

_____

_____

3. Not only was the Samaritan woman a victim of prejudice, she was also thoroughly steeped in religious and ethnic resentments of her own. Describe how Jesus dispelled prejudice in each of the following areas:

The woman's religious and ethnic biases (4:7–15).

_____

_____

_____

Her insecurity regarding her intimate relationships (4:16–18).

_____

_____

_____

Controversy over the correct place and manner of worship (4:19–26).

_____

_____

_____

4. List several results of Jesus' willingness to overcome the religious and cultural barriers that separated the Jews and Samaritans.

_____

_____

_____

5. What patterns can you see in Jesus' encounter with the woman at the well that might help you cross invisible lines of prejudice in your workplace?

_____

_____

_____

_____

_____

◆ Breaking Barriers ◆

In every workplace, tension sometimes exists between coworkers who approach life from different perspectives. Maybe you are in the midst of a prejudicial situation right now. If not, one day soon you probably will be. Why? Unfortunately, that is the type of world in which we live; someone is suspect if his or her skin color, ethnic background, language, clothing, or hairstyle is different from our own.

Many social scientists are throwing up their hands in despair, crying out, "What can we do? We've tried everything to relieve racial tensions in our streets and in our workplaces, and the problems continue to intensify. Why can't we all just get along?"

Ironically, the one Answer that offers hope of a true transformation—a relationship with Jesus Christ—is being ignored. Worse yet, many people in our society now regard Christians with an antagonism unparalleled since the days of the early church. But never fear! Historically, when the obstacles have been the most formidable, the Christian witness has been the most powerful. It hasn't always been easy, but where believers have obeyed His commands, they have turned barriers of opposition into bridges of opportunity.

 Acts 1:4–14

⁴And being assembled together with *them,* He commanded them not to depart from Jerusalem, but to wait for the Promise of the Father, "which," *He said,* "you have heard from Me; ⁵for John truly baptized with water, but you shall be baptized with the Holy Spirit not many days from now." ⁶Therefore, when they had come together, they asked Him, saying, "Lord, will You at this time restore the kingdom to Israel?" ⁷And He said to them, "It is not for you to know times or seasons which the Father has put in His own authority. ⁸But you shall receive power when the Holy Spirit has come upon you; and you shall be witnesses to Me in Jerusalem, and in all Judea and Samaria, and to the end of the earth."

⁹Now when He had spoken these things, while they watched, He was taken up, and a cloud received Him out of their sight. ¹⁰And while they looked steadfastly toward heaven as He went up, behold, two men stood by them in white apparel, ¹¹who also said, "Men of Galilee, why do you stand gazing up into heaven? This *same* Jesus, who was taken up from you into heaven, will so come in like manner as you saw Him go into heaven."

¹²Then they returned to Jerusalem from the mount called Olivet, which is near Jerusalem, a Sabbath day's journey. ¹³And when they had entered, they went up into the upper room where they were staying: Peter, James, John, and Andrew; Philip and Thomas; Bartholomew and Matthew; James *the son* of Alphaeus and Simon the Zealot; and Judas *the son* of James. ¹⁴These all continued with one accord in prayer and supplication, with the women and Mary the mother of Jesus, and with His brothers.

OPPORTUNITIES LOOK LIKE BARRIERS

A Grand Strategy

Speaking on the Mount of Olives at Bethany (Acts 1:4, 12), Jesus outlined a vision that would affect the whole world (1:8). He began by pointing to the starting point of gospel penetration—Jerusalem, two miles to the west. From there the message would spread to the surrounding region, Judea, and its estranged cousin to the north, Samaria. Eventually it would reach the entire world (though the crowd in Acts 1 probably understood "the end of the earth" as meaning the extent of the Roman Empire).

While Jesus' mandate sounds admirable today, it probably met with less than enthusiasm then. All of the places mentioned represented trouble and danger, both real and imagined. Jews—which almost all of Jesus' listeners were—were a small minority in the Roman Empire.

In fact, most of the apostles came from the Galilee region, north of Samaria. Galileans endured the scorn of their Jewish brothers from Judea, especially those from Jerusalem, who considered themselves more pure and orthodox, less contaminated by foreign influences. The lake region was derided as "Galilee of the Gentiles." Even the Galilean accent was chided.

Jerusalem

Jerusalem was not the apostles' home, but it was Judea's key

the place of greatest hostility and intimidation. They must have wondered: Could He protect them from the inevitable opposition they would encounter? Would they suffer the same terrible end that He had?

Judea and Samaria

The relationship of Jerusalem to Judea was that of urban center to province, or of city to state. By penetrating the city, the gospel would also permeate the city's surroundings.

THE SPREAD OF THE GOSPEL

city, center of its religious, political, economic, and cultural life. Jesus' crucifixion had recently taken place there. Leaders still plotted to stamp out what was left of His movement.

Yet Christ told His followers to start their witness there, in

However, Jesus was careful to link Judea to Samaria, its cousin to the north. The two regions endured a bitter rivalry dating to the seventh century B.C., when the Assyrians colonized Samaria with non-Jews who intermarried

continued

continued

with Israelites and thereby "corrupted" the race. Judea, which means "Jewish," considered itself the home of pure Judaism and viewed Samaria with contempt. As John points out in his account of the woman at the well at Sychar, "Jews have no dealings with Samaritans" (John 4:9).

In reaching Judea with the gospel, the Galilean apostles would have to surmount barriers of regional pride and cultural arrogance. But in moving into Samaria, they would have to overcome long-held ethnic prejudices.

The End of the Earth

Talk of the gospel spreading to "the end of the earth" signaled the eventual inclusion of Gentiles—the ultimate shock to the apostles. In their mind, the world was divided into Jews and non-Jews (Gentiles or "foreigners"). Extremely orthodox Jews would have nothing to do with Gentiles. Even Jews like the apostles, who had grown up alongside of Gentiles, avoided contact as much as possible.

For the gospel to spread to the Gentiles, then, Jesus' followers would have to overcome centuries of racial, religious, and cultural prejudice and break down well-established walls of separation. Eventually they did—but not without great conflict and tension. ◆

1. In Christ's lifetime, the cultured sophisticates in the city of Jerusalem looked down on the working-class apostles with Galilean accents. What accents receive the most criticism or ridicule in your workplace?

_____ Southern
_____ Boston
_____ New York
_____ New Jersey
_____ California
_____ Midwestern
_____ Spanish
_____ Canadian

2. How involved are you in Jesus' grand strategy to reach the world? Check those statements that best reflect your attitude and involvement.

_____ I am running for school board, city council, or other positions of service so I can bring Christian values to the public forum.
_____ I attend church.
_____ Hey, we have churches on every corner in this town! If people want to find out about Jesus, they can go to church.
_____ I am working in my county, state, or province with other believers to elect public officials who will reflect biblical values in our society.
_____ If something doesn't affect our town, I'm not interested. Let somebody else worry about it.
_____ I am ready to go wherever God calls me to represent Him.
_____ I support missionary and evangelistic efforts financially and prayerfully.

3a. What kinds of rivalries or tensions currently exist within your workplace?

_____

_____

_____

_____

_____

3b. In your opinion, what causes most of these tensions?

_____

_____

_____

_____

_____

3c. How do you usually deal with these tensions?

_____ I ignore them.
_____ I do my job and go home.
_____ I take the side of the offended party.
_____ I side with my friends, no matter who is right.
_____ I fight.
_____ I preach.
_____ I try to do whatever I think Jesus would do.

4. How can you help break down the walls of bitterness and separation that exist in your workplace?

_____

_____

_____

_____

_____

_____

ETHNIC WALLS BREAK DOWN

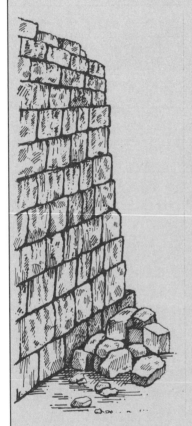

A major breakthrough in race relations is described in Acts 10. For years a virtual wall between Jews and Gentiles had hampered the apostles in sharing Jesus with the Gentile world. But when Peter met Cornelius—an officer of Rome's occupation troops in Palestine—two conversions took place: Cornelius, his family, and his friends came to faith; and Peter came to realize that God wants Gentiles in the church.

God easily could have used Philip the evangelist (Acts 8:5) to bring the gospel to Cornelius. After all, he lived in Caesarea and had already shown his willingness to share the gospel across ethnic lines. But no, God called Peter to bring His message to the Roman centurion. Apparently He wanted to break down barriers against Gentiles in Peter's heart.

How Peter Saw Cornelius

- *Living in Caesarea,* Roman military capital of Palestine (10:1).
- *A centurion,* commander of 100 occupying Roman troops (10:1).
- *Of the Italian Regiment,* all men from Italy (10:1).
- *Gentile* (10:1).
- *Unclean,* like the unclean animals of the Old Testament dietary laws (10:11–16).
- *Unlawful for a Jew to visit,* as he was from another nation (10:28).
- *Uncircumcised,* therefore not right to eat with (11:3).

In Peter's mind, these factors disqualified Cornelius from serving him dinner, let alone coming to faith. But Peter was following a "Jewish gospel."

God's intention had been that Hebrews would treat their Gentile neighbors cordially (Num. 35:15; Deut. 10:19; Ezek. 47:2). Of course, He also charged His people to exclude heathen practices,

continued

continued

particularly idolatry (Lev. 18:24—19:4; Deut. 12:29–31). Intermarriage was condemned, though sometimes allowed (compare Ex. 34:16; Deut. 7:3; Ezra 9:12; 10:2–44; Neh. 10:30). But the main concern was moral purity.

Through rabbinic tradition strict separation became the rule. By Peter's day, four hundred years of Greek and Roman oppression had only hardened Jewish resolve to avoid as much contact as possible with foreigners.

Peter and the other Jewish believers brought these attitudes with them into the church, which made it almost impossible for them to reach out to Gentiles.

How God Saw Cornelius

- *Devout* (10:2).
- *A God-fearer,* along with his household (10:2).
- *Generous to the poor* (10:2).
- *A man of prayer* whose prayers and alms were received by God (10:2, 4).
- *Obedient to God's angel* (10:7–8).
- *Cleansed by God,* so not unclean (10:15).
- *Crucial for Peter to visit* (10:5, 19–20).

God's view of Cornelius was a contrast to Peter's. Because of Christ, God was ready to throw the doors of faith wide open to Gentiles: "What God has cleansed you must not call common," He sternly declared to Peter (vv. 9–16). Because of Christ, the centurion could be "cleansed" from sin and be acceptable to God.

But Peter was confused. Should he break with his culture and visit this Gentile, violating traditional codes handed down as if carrying the force of God's law? He had at least two days to sort out his thoughts as he walked to Caesarea to meet Cornelius. His emotional struggle can be seen in his first words to the assembled group:

"You know how unlawful it is for a Jewish man to keep company with or go to one of another nation" (v. 28).

But God broke down the wall in Peter's heart by pouring out the Holy Spirit on these Gentile believers (vv. 44–45).

Peter's New Perspective

- "In truth I perceive that *God shows no partiality*" (10:34, italics added).
- "But *in every nation* whoever fears Him . . . is accepted by Him" (10:35, italics added).
- "Jesus Christ . . . is Lord of *all*" (10:36, italics added).
- "*Whoever believes* in Him will receive remission of sins" (10:43, italics added).
- "Can *anyone* forbid water, that *these* should not be baptized who have received the Holy Spirit *just as we have?*" (10:47, italics added).
- "God gave *them* the *same gift* as He gave us when we believed" (11:17, italics added).
- "*Who was I* that I could withstand God?" (11:17, italics added).

Breaking Down Barriers Today

Attitudes of prejudice and legalism trouble the church today just as they did the early church. Believers sometimes mingle cultural biases with biblical mandates, creating wrenching controversies over numerous sensitive issues. Certainly issues need to be addressed, particularly when essentials of the faith are at stake. But one of those biblical essentials is that believers eagerly seek out *all* people, look at them from God's perspective, love them for the gospel's sake, and rejoice over those that respond in faith. Can the church ever afford to wall itself off through fear or prejudice? Doing so would be to turn away from God's compassionate heart. ◆

Acts 10:1–48

¹There was a certain man in Caesarea called Cornelius, a centurion of what was called the Italian Regiment, ²a devout *man* and one who feared God with all his household, who gave alms generously to the people, and prayed to God always. ³About the ninth hour of the day he saw clearly in a vision an angel of God coming in and saying to him, "Cornelius!"

⁴And when he observed him, he was afraid, and said, "What is it, lord?"

So he said to him, "Your prayers and your alms have come up for a memorial before God. ⁵Now send men to Joppa, and send for Simon whose surname is Peter. ⁶He is lodging with Simon, a tanner, whose house is by the sea. He will tell you what you must do." ⁷And when the angel who spoke to him had departed, Cornelius called two of his household servants and a devout soldier from among those who waited on him continually. ⁸So when he had explained all *these* things to them, he sent them to Joppa.

⁹The next day, as they went on their journey and drew near the city, Peter went up on the housetop to pray, about the sixth hour. ¹⁰Then he became very hungry and wanted to eat; but while they made ready, he fell into a trance ¹¹and saw heaven opened and an object like a great sheet bound at the four corners, descending to him and let down to the earth. ¹²In it were all kinds of four-footed animals of the earth, wild beasts, creeping things, and birds of the air. ¹³And a voice came to him, "Rise, Peter; kill and eat."

¹⁴But Peter said, "Not so, Lord! For I have never eaten anything common or unclean."

¹⁵And a voice *spoke* to him again the second time, "What God has cleansed you must not call common." ¹⁶This was done three times. And the object was taken up into heaven again.

¹⁷Now while Peter wondered within himself what this vision which he had seen meant, behold, the men who had been sent from Cornelius had made inquiry for Simon's house, and stood before the gate. ¹⁸And they called and asked whether Simon, whose surname was Peter, was lodging there.

¹⁹While Peter thought about the vision, the Spirit said to him, "Behold, three men are seeking you. ²⁰Arise therefore, go down and go with them, doubting nothing; for I have sent them."

²¹Then Peter went down to the men who had been sent to him from Cornelius, and said, "Yes, I am he whom you seek. For what reason have you come?"

²²And they said, "Cornelius *the* centurion, a just man, one who fears God and has a good reputation among all the nation of the Jews, was divinely instructed by a holy angel to summon you to his house, and to hear words from you." ²³Then he invited them in and lodged *them*.

On the next day Peter went away with them, and some brethren from Joppa accompanied him.

²⁴And the following day they entered Caesarea. Now Cornelius was waiting for them, and had called together his relatives and close friends. ²⁵As Peter was coming in, Cornelius met him and fell down at his feet and worshiped *him*. ²⁶But Peter lifted him up, saying, "Stand up; I myself am also a man." ²⁷And as he talked with him, he went in and found many who had come together. ²⁸Then he said to them, "You know how unlawful it is for a Jewish man to keep company with or go to one of another nation. But God has shown me that I should not call any man common or unclean. ²⁹Therefore I came without objection as soon as I was sent for. I ask, then, for what reason have you sent for me?"

³⁰So Cornelius said, "Four days ago I was fasting until this hour; and at the ninth hour I prayed in my house, and behold, a man stood before me in bright clothing, ³¹and said, 'Cornelius, your prayer has been heard, and your alms are remembered in the sight of God. ³²Send therefore to Joppa and call Simon here, whose surname is Peter. He is lodging in the house of Simon, a tanner, by the sea. When he comes, he will speak to you.'

continued

continued

³³So I sent to you immediately, and you have done well to come. Now therefore, we are all present before God, to hear all the things commanded you by God."

³⁴Then Peter opened *his* mouth and said: "In truth I perceive that God shows no partiality. ³⁵But in every nation whoever fears Him and works righteousness is accepted by Him. ³⁶The word which *God* sent to the children of Israel, preaching peace through Jesus Christ—He is Lord of all— ³⁷that word you know, which was proclaimed throughout all Judea, and began from Galilee after the baptism which John preached: ³⁸how God anointed Jesus of Nazareth with the Holy Spirit and with power, who went about doing good and healing all who were oppressed by the devil, for God was with Him. ³⁹And we are witnesses of all things which He did both in the land of the Jews and in Jerusalem, whom they killed by hanging on a tree. ⁴⁰Him God raised up on the third day, and showed Him openly, ⁴¹not to all the people, but to witnesses chosen before by God, *even* to us who ate and drank with Him after He arose from the dead. ⁴²And He commanded us to preach to the people, and to testify that it is He who was ordained by God *to be* Judge of the living and the dead. ⁴³To Him all the prophets witness that, through His name, whoever believes in Him will receive remission of sins."

⁴⁴While Peter was still speaking these words, the Holy Spirit fell upon all those who heard the word. ⁴⁵And those of the circumcision who believed were astonished, as many as came with Peter, because the gift of the Holy Spirit had been poured out on the Gentiles also. ⁴⁶For they heard them speak with tongues and magnify God.

Then Peter answered, ⁴⁷"Can anyone forbid water, that these should not be baptized who have received the Holy Spirit just as we *have?*" ⁴⁸And he commanded them to be baptized in the name of the Lord. Then they asked him to stay a few days.

---

1. Do you remember when you were a child and your parents made you visit some friends or relatives you didn't particularly like or with whom you had little in common? How did you feel about your visit? (For instance: I felt extremely uncomfortable; I resented my weird relatives.)

_____

_____

2a. Do you think Peter would have visited Cornelius's home if God had not spoken to him so directly (10:14–16)?

_____ Yes   _____ No

2b. How would you respond if you had a dream in which a voice told you that you should cross one of the racial, cultural, or ethnic lines in your workplace to share the gospel with someone?

_____

_____

3. Three times Peter saw a vision of ritually unclean animals, and each time a heavenly voice commanded Peter to go against his Jewish convictions (10:9–16). What do you think God was showing Peter through these visions?

_____

_____

_____

4a. What incredible realization did Peter come to as a result of his encounter with Cornelius?

_____

_____

4b. How does this information relate to your attitude toward your coworkers whose ethnic backgrounds, educational levels, languages, work habits, or cultures are different from your own?

_____

_____

———◆ That's What It's All About ◆———

A GREAT MULTITUDE OF ALL NATIONS

Jesus sent His followers to make disciples of all the nations (*ethnē*, "peoples"). As John takes us into the throne room of heaven, we see the fulfillment of Jesus' mandate. There, standing before the Lamb (Christ) is a crowd so large that it cannot be counted, made up of "all nations, tribes, peoples, and tongues" (Rev. 7:9).

Actually, two groups are present—representatives from God's people, the Jews (7:3–8), and countless Gentile believers (7:9–10). Just as Jesus said it would, the gospel has spread out from Jerusalem to reach people from "the end of the earth" (Acts 1:8). Now Jews and Gentiles have come together to receive the salvation that God has promised. Now God dwells among His people. Jesus is their Shepherd, supplying all their needs (Rev. 7:14–17).

In response to this spectacular, worldwide, multiethnic salvation, the creatures of heaven and earth fall down before God in worship and song (vv. 11–12). What a breathtaking picture this is!

But of course this vision lies in the future. For now, we live in a world wracked by ethnic divisions and racial prejudice. Yet knowing that God intends to populate heaven with people from every ethnic background has important implications for those of us who claim to follow Christ. If God's heart reaches out to the whole world, then our hearts need to as well.

Revelation 7:9–17

⁹After these things I looked, and behold, a great multitude which no one could number, of all nations, tribes, peoples, and tongues, standing before the throne and before the Lamb, clothed with white robes, with palm branches in their hands, ¹⁰and crying out with a loud voice, saying, "Salvation *belongs* to our God who sits on the throne, and to the Lamb!" ¹¹All the angels stood around the throne and the elders and the four living creatures, and fell on their faces before the throne and worshiped God, ¹²saying:

> "Amen! Blessing and glory and wisdom,
> Thanksgiving and honor and power and
>   might,
> *Be* to our God forever and ever.
> Amen."

¹³Then one of the elders answered, saying to me, "Who are these arrayed in white robes, and where did they come from?"

¹⁴And I said to him, "Sir, you know."

So he said to me, "These are the ones who come out of the great tribulation, and washed their robes and made them white in the blood of the Lamb. ¹⁵Therefore they are before the throne of God, and serve Him day and night in His temple. And He who sits on the throne will dwell among them. ¹⁶They shall neither hunger anymore nor thirst anymore; the sun shall not strike them, nor any heat; ¹⁷for the Lamb who is in the midst of the throne will shepherd them and lead them to living fountains of waters. And God will wipe away every tear from their eyes."

1. How does knowing that you will spend eternity with people from every race, color, culture, and ethnic background affect your attitude toward those who are different from you?

_____

_____

_____

2. Various Bible scholars hold different opinions concerning who the people are that comprise the great multitude mentioned in Revelation 7:9. Two characteristics of this multitude, however, are beyond question:

They have been completely forgiven (7:14).
They remained faithful to Jesus Christ, even in times of awful tribulation (7:14).

How do these two characteristics relate to you? (For instance: I have repented of my sins and Christ has forgiven me.)

_____

_____

_____

3. Complete the following statement:

(Name) _____ has hurt me or offended me, but today (date), _____ because Christ has forgiven me, I choose to forgive my offender.

◆ ◆ ◆ ◆ ◆ ◆ ◆ ◆ ◆

It takes real courage to cross cultural barriers within the workplace. Some of your friends and coworkers may not understand your actions, or they may misinterpret your motives. But the risk will be worth it. After all, if anyone should lead the way in breaking down barriers established by attitudes of prejudice and bias, it is the believer in the workplace. Don't be afraid to take that first step along "the road less traveled." Jesus will meet you there and will walk with you every step of the way.

If we commit ourselves to Christ, and repent of our presumption, pride, and prejudice, God will revitalize our own spiritual lives. He will also give us a fresh understanding of His desire to bring people of every race, color, and background into His "forever family." That in itself should motivate us to tear down walls that divide us.

Furthermore, as we begin actively reaching out to other people and building bridges to those of different traditions, we will discover that what binds us together is stronger than what divides us. We can join in a common mission of taking the good news of Jesus outside our churches, into our homes and workplaces, and into the streets of our cities.

After all, both Jesus and the apostle Paul incorporated a method of operation in which they impacted the heavily populated areas as well as the rural areas. Today, many exciting new ministries are springing up in the suburbs. But, are we overlooking a diamond in the rough in the cities? We'll find out in our next chapter.

At Work in Your City

Do you remember when you knew most of the people in your neighborhood? It seems as though it were just yesterday, doesn't it? You could walk down the street and wave to folks as they hung out their laundry or did their yard work. You greeted people by name when you passed them on the sidewalk.

If you had car trouble, old Joe down at the garage would fix you up—and he didn't overcharge you. Broken water pipes after the big freeze? No problem; just call Al at the hardware store. He and his boys would be right over. The furnace went out? Don't worry; Al does furnaces too.

Things were different in the workplace, too. Coworkers used to come from somewhat similar backgrounds. Although they may have been culturally and ethnically diverse, they still had a similar work ethic— a fair day's work for a fair wage. Many people worked at the same job for most of their adult lives, and those who did change jobs made minimal career moves. As a result, coworkers often knew each other rather well. They knew about each other's families and their beliefs. They socialized together outside the workplace and often attended the same church.

But times have changed.

With the advent of television, computers, modems, fax machines, and the "information superhighway," we no longer live in small-town neighborhoods. We now live in global communities. Furthermore, because of the population explosion, many of our small towns have disappeared. Oh, they still exist on the map, but most small towns have been snatched up by the all-consuming tentacles of the big cities.

And, with the increased population comes an increase in crime, pollution, taxes, and traffic, accompanied by a corresponding decrease in community interaction and genuine caring for and communication with our neighbors. Nowadays, most of us are emotionally closer to someone who lives five hundred to a thousand miles away than we are to anyone who lives in our neighborhood.

Nevertheless, the cities have many positive qualities. Employment and educational opportunities are usually greater in a metropolitan area. Cultural, social, artistic, and entertainment programs are also easier to find in the cities. Churches are greater in number and diversity in a large city. And, the opportunity to share the good news of Jesus Christ is greater in the city.

Maybe that is why Jesus focused so much of His ministry on urban centers, and why He directed His disciples to do the same. If you have always thought of Jesus as "just a country preacher," the next article may surprise you!

JESUS—A CITY PREACHER

Popular opinion frequently regards the Bible in general and the ministry of Jesus in particular in rural terms. Perhaps it's the Christmas story, with its quaint references to a donkey, a manger, and shepherds. Perhaps it's the memorable parables, such as the sower and the seed, the wheat and the weeds, and the prodigal son. Perhaps it's Jesus' origins in a small town. Whatever the cause, the popular image of Jesus and His world seems fixed on a rural environment. But that is somewhat misleading.

Palestine in Jesus' day was undergoing rapid urban development. Its population of around 2.5 to 3 million people lived in numerous preindustrial cities and towns that revolved around Jerusalem, the hub of the region. The Holy City had a population conservatively estimated by modern scholars at between 55,000 and 90,000. (Josephus, a first-century Jewish historian, placed the number at 3 million; the Talmud gives an incredible 12 million.)

So as Jesus carried out His ministry, He focused on the urban centers of Palestine (Matt. 9:35; 11:1; Luke 4:43; 13:22) and visited Jerusalem at least three times. This brought Him into contact with a greater number and wider variety of people than He would have encountered in a purely rural campaign—women, soldiers, religious leaders, the rich,

merchants, tax collectors, Gentiles, prostitutes, beggars, and the poor. These He attracted in large crowds as He visited each city.

Jesus' urban strategy established a model for His disciples and the early church. When He sent the disciples on preaching tours, He directed them toward cities (Matt. 10:5, 11–14; Luke 10:1, 8–16). And later, the movement spread throughout the Roman empire by using an urban strategy that planted communities of believers in no less than 40 cities by the end of the first century.

In light of the vital role that cities played in the ministry of Jesus, we who follow Him today need to ask: What are we doing to relate the message of Christ to our increasingly urban, multicultural, and pluralistic world? Our Lord's example in urban Palestine has much to teach us. ◆

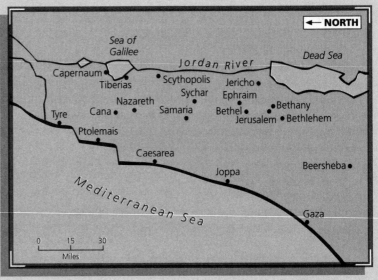

CITIES OF PALESTINE IN CHRIST'S TIME

Matthew 9:35–38

³⁵Then Jesus went about all the cities and villages, teaching in their synagogues, preaching the gospel of the kingdom, and healing every sickness and every disease among the people. ³⁶But when He saw the multitudes, He was moved with compassion for them, because they were weary and scattered, like sheep having no shepherd. ³⁷Then He said to His disciples, "The harvest truly *is* plentiful, but the laborers *are* few. ³⁸Therefore pray the Lord of the harvest to send out laborers into His harvest."

◆ ◆ ◆ ◆ ◆ ◆ ◆ ◆ ◆

1a. What three things do you enjoy most about the city you live in or near?

1b. What three things do you dislike the most about this city?

2. In Matthew 9:36, Jesus was moved with compassion when He saw the multitudes like sheep without a shepherd. Describe how you think Jesus might view the multitudes in your city (or the city closest to you).

3. What do you think Jesus meant when He said, "The harvest truly is plentiful, but the laborers are few" (9:37)?

4. Why do you think Jesus asks us to pray that the Lord will send out more laborers? Why doesn't He just send them whether we ask or not?

_____

_____

_____

_____

——◆ But What Can I Do? ◆——

When Jesus asks you to become a worker with Him, He does not request that you quit your job and join a missions group (although He might!). Relatively few people are actually called to abandon their professions to follow Jesus. More frequently, He seeks people who will have the courage to stand up and be counted as His representatives wherever they are. He is calling us to develop a Christlike mind-set and to model a Christlike lifestyle.

It's one thing to adopt Christlike behavior by reaching out to family and friends. It is another story to try to reach out to strangers. There are so many problems, how can we possibly make a difference?

People become apathetic because they know so much about the world, they are overwhelmed. They believe that as individuals they do not matter. It is easy to fall into an apathetic trap and develop a mind-set of, "Sure, I care; but what can I do about it?"

- "What can I do about the homeless people?"
- "What can I do about world hunger, or even the people who are malnourished in my city?"
- "What can I do to help AIDS victims?"
- "What can I do about a faltering economy?"
- "What can I do about crime in our streets?"
- "What can I do about teenage pregnancies?"

With this plethora of problems facing us, it is no wonder people get depressed. Perhaps, the real miracle is that more people are not despondent! But the good news is that everybody you meet is just as baffled and troubled about these problems as you are. When you muster the tiniest bit of faith and step into the world in an effort to help make things better, you will find that the step you have taken leads right into the hearts of hurting, hungry people. Hearts that are hungry to know God. And you can make a difference!

We all have a stirring in our hearts at one time or another, urging us to do something to help the suffering and the needy people around us. Those impulses should not be ignored. Someone once asked Mother Teresa of Calcutta how she got started in her mission of mercy. The diminutive woman replied, "If I had not picked up that first person dying on the street, I would not have picked up the thousands later on."

Maybe you can't save thousands of people who are dying in the streets or help feed millions of starving people, but you may be able to help one. Maybe you can't visit everyone *who is alone in a hospital or nursing home, but there is a lonely woman or man somewhere in your city who is looking out the window right now, longing for someone to come and share a little love with them. You can be that someone!*

Maybe you can't stop all the violence in the streets. But there are people in your workplace and in your community who desperately need to hear about the peace of Christ, which will allow them to sleep securely at night—peace that doesn't come from bombs, missiles, a bottle, or drugs.

PEOPLE PRIORITIES IN THE CITY

Believers today can feel overwhelmed as they look at the many needs in the world around them. Where should they start? How can they make any difference? Who needs help the most?

Jesus modeled several lessons in dealing with the needs of people when He disembarked from His sail across the Sea of Galilee (Mark 5:21). He found Himself confronted by two individuals with critical needs: a well-off, well-connected, and well-respected synagogue ruler whose twelve-year-old daughter was terminally ill (vv. 22–24); and an obscure elderly woman who had spent her livelihood on an ineffectual medical system, yet still suffered from chronic bleeding (vv. 25–28).

The man, with all his connections, got to Jesus first. But as Jesus was on His way across town, the woman—unnamed, unannounced, and, from the crowd's point of view, unwanted—grabbed Him. It was the desperate act of someone who knew she was going to die unless a miracle of some sort took place.

A little girl who had been living for twelve years (v. 42) and an old lady who had been dying for twelve years (v. 25). What would Jesus do?

To complicate matters, the woman's touch rendered Jesus ritually unclean (Lev. 15:25–27). Technically, He was now prohibited from helping the little girl until the next day. But neither the woman nor Jesus cared about that in the least: she was more amazed at her immediate healing, and Jesus was aware that His power had been activated (vv. 29–30). He was able to distinguish the incidental touch of the crowd from the person who reached out in faith.

Jesus called her "daughter" (v. 34). Perhaps He was referring to her Jewish ancestry. He called a woman in a similar situation a daughter of Abraham (Luke 13:16). But the

continued

continued

term also put her on an equal footing with the daughter of the ruler—and put Jesus in sympathy with Jairus as a parent in pain. Perhaps that's why Jairus continued to trust Jesus even as his crisis worsened (vv. 35–36).

No individual Christian can meet all the des-perate needs in today's urban arena. But does God really ask us to? If Jesus' example in Mark 5 is any indication, we need to do what we can to re-spond to the individuals *He sends our way. We also need to remember that chronically ill old ladies mean just as much to God as bright, privi-leged schoolgirls.* ◆

Mark 5:21–43

21Now when Jesus had crossed over again by boat to the other side, a great multitude gathered to Him; and He was by the sea. 22And behold, one of the rulers of the synagogue came, Jairus by name. And when he saw Him, he fell at His feet 23and begged Him earnestly, saying, "My little daughter lies at the point of death. Come and lay Your hands on her, that she may be healed, and she will live." 24So *Jesus* went with him, and a great multitude followed Him and thronged Him.

25Now a certain woman had a flow of blood for twelve years, 26and had suffered many things from many physicians. She had spent all that she had and was no better, but rather grew worse. 27When she heard about Jesus, she came behind *Him* in the crowd and touched His garment. 28For she said, "If only I may touch His clothes, I shall be made well."

29Immediately the fountain of her blood was dried up, and she felt in *her* body that she was healed of the affliction. 30And Jesus, immediately knowing in Himself that power had gone out of Him, turned around in the crowd and said, "Who touched My clothes?"

31But His disciples said to Him, "You see the multitude thronging You, and You say, 'Who touched Me?' "

32And He looked around to see her who had done this thing. 33But the woman, fearing and trembling, knowing what had happened to her, came and fell down before Him and told Him the whole truth. 34And He said to her, "Daughter, your faith has made you well. Go in peace, and be healed of your affliction."

35While He was still speaking, *some* came from the ruler of the synagogue's *house* who said, "Your daughter is dead. Why trouble the Teacher any further?"

36As soon as Jesus heard the word that was spoken, He said to the ruler of the synagogue, "Do not be afraid; only believe." 37And He permitted no one to follow Him except Peter, James, and John the brother of James. 38Then He came to the house of the ruler of the synagogue, and saw a tumult and those who wept and wailed loudly. 39When He came in, He said to them, "Why make this commotion and weep? The child is not dead, but sleeping."

40And they ridiculed Him. But when He had put them all outside, He took the father and the mother of the child, and those *who were* with Him, and entered where the child was lying. 41Then He took the child by the hand, and said to her, "Talitha, cumi," which is translated, "Little girl, I say to you, arise." 42Immediately the girl arose and walked, for she was twelve years *of age*. And they were overcome with great amazement. 43But He commanded them strictly that no one should know it, and said that *something* should be given her to eat.

1. What do you suppose Jairus was thinking when the woman with the hemorrhage interrupted him and Jesus on their way to Jairus' nearly dead daughter?

_____

_____

_____

_____

2. Both Jairus (5:22) and the woman (5:33) fell at Jesus' feet as they spoke to Him. What do you think that indicates about their attitudes toward Jesus?

_____

_____

_____

_____

3. As Jesus and Jairus moved through the crowd, most likely they were being jostled and bumped by the people. When the woman with the hemorrhage touched Jesus' garment, He instantly knew it. How do you think He knew?

_____

_____

_____

_____

4. Hundreds of needs were represented in the crowd that day, yet, as far as we know, Jesus healed only two individuals. How can Jesus' actions affect your attitude toward the vast needs in today's society?

_____

_____

_____

_____

5. Jesus' words to Jairus, "Do not be afraid; only believe" (5:36), are drenched with hope. What situations in your life cause you to need Jesus to speak those same words to you? (For instance, my relationship with my spouse or my financial needs.)

_____

_____

_____

_____

_____

_____

◆ Do Something Beautiful for God ◆

Not long after Mother Teresa opened the Home for the Dying among the one million destitute, diseased refugees who had flocked to Calcutta, Eileen Egan, Mother Teresa's friend, visited the unassuming nun. The western woman was shocked as she walked with Mother Teresa through the teeming masses of impoverished people. The westerner had not imagined the dire circumstances in which Mother Teresa was working. Squalor and death surrounded

them everywhere they went.

In the midst of this seemingly hopeless situation, Mother Teresa had opened the home to bring healing to the skeletal human beings who could be helped, and dignity to those whose deaths were imminent. Each day Mother Teresa's friend followed the nun as she made her rounds from pallet to pallet. Each day, more forsaken human beings were brought to the home to have the filth of the gutter washed off their bodies, and to

have their sores cleaned and bandaged. The painfully slow parade of nearly dead bodies never stopped during the westerner's visit.

Finally, the woman asked Mother Teresa, "How can you do this day after day?"

The modern-day saint smiled faintly at her friend and answered in words that have become famous among those familiar with Mother Teresa's work. "They are Jesus," she replied. "Each one is Jesus in a distressing disguise."

◆ ◆ ◆ ◆ ◆ ◆ ◆ ◆ ◆

Jesus made a point of reaching out to people that society had rejected, ignored, or ostracized. Naturally, the common and impoverished people heard Him gladly. They still do today. Whenever someone has the courage to share the love of Christ with them, they see the work of Christ. What is your attitude toward your city's underclass? ◆

THE UNDERCLASS

Nearly every society and every city in biblical times had a large underclass—people scraping by on the margins of society. Tending to congregate in the cities, the underclass included the poor, the sick, the disabled, the lepers, the blind, the insane, the demon-possessed, widows, orphans, runaways, castaways, and refugees. Lacking resources to provide for even their basic needs, many turned to begging, stealing, menial labor, slavery, and prostitution. Few cultures made provision for these desperate, destitute wanderers, and so they remained largely powerless to change their condition.

Yet it was to the underclass that Jesus intentionally directed much of His life and ministry. They were among the "blessed" in His opening remarks in the Sermon on the Mount (Matt. 5:3–10). And He declared that He had come to bring them good news in his inaugural sermon at Nazareth (Luke 4:17–18). So it was no surprise that when John's questioning disciples came to ask whether He was indeed the Messiah, they found Him ministering among the underclass (Luke 7:20–21).

Nor was it any surprise that the early church continued this outreach. They used their resources to meet material needs among their own members (Acts 2:44–45; 4:32, 34–35). They attracted the sick and afflicted (5:12–16). They appointed leaders to manage social programs for widows (6:1–6). They sent famine relief (11:27–30). They urged new leaders to remember the poor (Gal. 2:10). They even evaluated their success in part by how much they collected in charitable contributions (Rom. 15:26–27).

To what extent will Christians today follow in the footsteps of Jesus and the first believers? Our cities, like theirs, are filling up with an underclass. How can we offer "good news" to them? Can we touch their bodies as well as their souls? Do we take them as seriously as our Savior did? ◆

Luke 7:20–23

²⁰When the men had come to Him, they said, "John the Baptist has sent us to You, saying, 'Are You the Coming One, or do we look for another?' " ²¹And that very hour He cured many of infirmities, afflictions, and evil spirits; and to many blind He gave sight.

²²Jesus answered and said to them, "Go and tell John the things you have seen and heard: that *the* blind see, *the* lame walk, *the* lepers are cleansed, *the* deaf hear, *the* dead are raised, *the* poor have the gospel preached to them. ²³And blessed is *he* who is not offended because of Me."

1. How do you think the believer's concern (or lack of concern) about society's underclass impacts welfare and other government assistance programs?

_____

_____

_____

_____

2. Many believers are reluctant to volunteer to serve in prison ministries or inner city ministries. How would you feel about being part of such a group? Check the response that most closely describes your own.

_____ I'd be excited about such an opportunity.
_____ I'd be reluctant to get involved. I would have difficulty sharing my faith in a hostile environment, but I might try.
_____ I don't function well in those kinds of circumstances. I'd refuse to get involved.

3. Why do you think John asked Jesus to confirm whether He was the Messiah?

_____

_____

_____

_____

4. How does Jesus' description of His ministry in Luke 7:22 prove that He is the Messiah?

_____

_____

_____

5. Members of the early church sacrificed their material possessions to help meet the needs of the poor, starving underclass among them. Name three things you would be willing to give up to help meet the needs in your community.

_____

_____

_____

—◆ A Church Ahead of Its Time ◆—

In the 1960s, President Lyndon Johnson and his political colleagues announced the establishment of "The Great Society." Their plan was to do away with racism, ethnic divisions, and poverty in America. The program was hailed by some as a revolutionary new idea. It wasn't, though. In fact, the church of Jesus Christ had been doing just that for over 1900 years, without destroying personal dignity or personal responsibility. Here's how the church did it.

ANTIOCH: A MODEL FOR THE MODERN CHURCH?

Even though first-century Christians made regular pilgrimages to Jerusalem and met annually in the upper room, the city of Antioch—not Jerusalem—was the center of early Christianity. In fact, modern churches might consider Antioch as a model for what God's people ought to be and do.

Like most cities today, Antioch was racially diverse and culturally pluralistic. As a result, when the scattered believers arrived there (Acts 11:19–20), they had to wrestle with how to make the gospel meaningful for a diversity of groups. Four factors help to account for their success.

(1) They saw ethnic division as a barrier to overcome rather than a status quo to be maintained. *Antioch walled off the four dominant ethnic groups of its population, Greek, Syrian, African, and Jewish. But the gospel breaks down walls of separation and hostility (Eph. 2:14–22) and brings diverse peoples together in Christ. We know that the Antioch believers broke through the ethnic barriers because . . .*

(2) They soon had multiethnic leadership. *The church employed and deployed pastors, teachers, and evangelists who reflected the composition of the community. Notice the cross-section of the city represented by the leadership team in Acts 13:1:*

- *Barnabas, a Hellenist from Cyprus raised in a priestly family. Appropriately, he was the first major leader of the new group (Acts 4:36; 11:22–23).*
- *Simeon (Niger), an African.*
- *Lucius of Cyrene, also of African descent.*
- *Manaen, a childhood companion of Herod Antipas (the ruler who killed John the Baptist, Mark 6:17–28), perhaps even a relative, and surely a privileged member of society.*

continued

continued

• *Saul, a Hellenistic Jew from Tarsus with rabbinical training who had Roman citizenship. Note how Barnabas intentionally recruited this young, untried leader for the work (Acts 11:25–26).*

(3) **They sent out ministry teams.** *Just as the church at Antioch had been established by believers fleeing from Jerusalem, it, too, sent out ministry teams to tell the story of Jesus. Paul used Antioch as his base of operation for three successive tours (13:1–3; 15:36–41; and 18:22–23). Moreover, Antioch served as a crossroads for travelers from the Tigris and Euphrates River valleys to the east, Asia Minor to the north, and Egypt to the south. So the church was able to maintain an international outreach in its own hometown.*

(4) **They joined together to accomplish projects of compassion.** *A famine in Judea became an opportunity for the multiethnic Christians at Antioch to serve their predominantly Jewish brothers in Judea (Acts 11:27–30). Paul recognized how powerful the "politics of compassion" could be at uniting otherwise disconnected churches. "Remember the poor" became his rallying cry to bring together believers in Ephesus, Corinth, Thessalonica, Galatia, and Rome with those at Jerusalem (Acts 20:17–18, 35; 2 Cor. 8:1—9:15; Gal. 2:10).*

Overall, Antioch became the model for how the church ought to function when surrounded by diversity and cultural pluralism. ◆

 Acts 13:1–3

¹Now in the church that was at Antioch there were certain prophets and teachers: Barnabas, Simeon who was called Niger, Lucius of Cyrene, Manaen who had been brought up with Herod the tetrarch, and Saul. ²As they ministered to the Lord and fasted, the Holy Spirit said, "Now separate to Me Barnabas and Saul for the work to which I have called them." ³Then, having fasted and prayed, and laid hands on them, they sent *them* away.

1. In your opinion, what changes will be necessary to have greater unity in your workplace? List two that you regard as important.

_____

_____

2. The multiethnic leadership in the early church was fairly effective at diffusing divisions within the Body of Christ. Look back at the article "Antioch: A Model For The Modern Church?" and notice the four keys to their success. Now, let's assume that you are a manager attempting to motivate your employees and create a greater sense of camaraderie in your workplace. Write a four-point plan based upon the Antioch church model that might help you accomplish your goals.

_____

_____

_____

_____

3. The church in Antioch grew rapidly as a result of many believers' fleeing Jerusalem after Stephen was martyred. God took what was a grave injustice and a tragedy and turned it into something wonderful. Describe a time in your life when God turned a tragedy into a triumph.

_____

_____

_____

4. The Antioch believers were blessed because they continually used their resources, their people, and their money to send out ministry teams to be blessings to others. List some practical ways you can bless someone else, thus showing gratitude to God for the way He has blessed you.

_____

_____

_____

——◆ A New Understanding ◆——

In many ways, the church at Antioch was the first experiment in cross-cultural Christianity. People from various racial, ethnic, and religious backgrounds came together to share their love for Christ. What an exciting group they must have been! Perhaps even more startling than the church's curious composition was its open acceptance of Gentile converts without making them adhere to ceremonial rites of the Jewish law. Unfettered from legalistic laws, the believers at Antioch allowed the Holy Spirit to gently guide them in the transition from being a church primarily composed of Jewish people, to a cosmopolitan body based upon Jewish foundations, which is now centered in Christ. But what should you call such a conglomeration?

A NEW REALITY GETS A NEW NAME

As Jesus' band of followers grew into a movement, they were called the Way (Acts 9:2), probably a reference to Christ's statement, "I am the Way" (John 14:6). For the most part, members of the Way had been Jewish believers.

But in Antioch there was an infusion of other ethnic groups, and observers were perplexed as to what to call the multicultural body. The new reality required a new name. Standard ethnic designations—Jews, Greeks, Romans, Gentiles—no longer fit. So the Antiochians seized on the one factor that united the diverse community—Christ. Actually, the term "Christians," or Christ-followers, was a sarcastic put-down (Acts 11:26). But the term stuck and even became a name of honor.

continued

continued

Are there perceptions of the faith where you live and work that are inadequate? Can you change some of those with a display of what following Christ actually involves? Are there ways in which coworkers, friends, or relatives can be touched by the faith, ways that will cause a breakthrough in understanding?

 Acts 11:22–26

22Then news of these things came to the ears of the church in Jerusalem, and they sent out Barnabas to go as far as Antioch. 23When he came and had seen the grace of God, he was glad, and encouraged them all that with purpose of heart they should continue with the Lord. 24For he was a good man, full of the Holy Spirit and of faith. And a great many people were added to the Lord. 25Then Barnabas departed for Tarsus to seek Saul. 26And when he had found him, he brought him to Antioch. So it was that for a whole year they assembled with the church and taught a great many people. And the disciples were first called Christians in Antioch.

1. What does the term *Christian* mean to you?

_____

_____

_____

2. Almost all religions encourage people "to be good." What makes Christianity different?

_____

_____

_____

_____

3. How can that difference transform the social fabric of your city?

_____

_____

_____

_____

Over half the world's population currently lives in cities. In California, for example, the percentage of the population living in urban centers is a stifling ninety percent. Many social scientists estimate that within the next decade, three of every four people in the world will live in cities. Clearly, the days of "small town USA" are gone.

But God loves cities, too! According to His Word, human history began in a garden, but it will end in a city—God's city! In the meantime, as believers in the workplace, we must learn to live and work in an environment that is extremely different from that in which we may have grown up. More than that, we must learn how to cross cultural lines to share our faith in Jesus Christ.

Brushing shoulders with people who do not share your cultural backgrounds may make you slightly uncomfortable. But go ahead, risk it. You might be surprised by what God will do in and through your life.

In this pluralistic society, you will be called upon increasingly to model what it means to be a genuine Christian. And, as your city and your workplace fill with a multiplicity of people, you can be sure somebody will be watching you to discern your concepts of success. What will you show them? What will you tell them? How does God measure success? In the following chapter, we're going to find out.

WHAT IS TRUE SUCCESS?

Would you consider this guy a success? As far as we know, he was never gainfully employed. He never had a bank account. He never dressed in fancy, designer suits. On the contrary, he clothed himself in camel's hair and a leather belt.

He never had a credit card, nor was he ever a member of a country club. But that's just as well; this fellow had fairly strange tastes in food. He wasn't into quiche, tofu, or fish eggs; he preferred eating grasshoppers and wild honey.

He was, however, quite an accomplished public speaker. Crowds came from everywhere to hear him, often braving extremely adverse conditions simply for the privilege of being in his audience. It's not that his messages were sugar-coated and easy to swallow. They weren't. In fact, many lawyers and religious leaders were offended by his hard-hitting, radical remarks. But then, how would you feel if someone called you and your friends a brood of snakes?

When he went so far as to insult the king of the land (to his face!), the rabble-rouser's career came to a screeching halt. The king had him tossed into prison and, at the urging of the queen, eventually had him executed.

A success? Surely not! Yet, Jesus said that there has never been another guy quite like him (Matt. 11:7–11). Obviously, John the Baptist knew something about true success that many of us have missed.

John 3:28–36

28"You yourselves bear me witness, that I said, 'I am not the Christ,' but, 'I have been sent before Him.' 29He who has the bride is the bridegroom; but the friend of the bridegroom, who stands and hears him, rejoices greatly because of the bridegroom's voice. Therefore this joy of mine is fulfilled. 30He must increase, but I *must* decrease. 31He who comes from above is above all; he who is of the earth is earthly and speaks of the earth. He who comes from heaven is above all.

32And what He has seen and heard, that He testifies; and no one receives His testimony. 33He who has received His testimony has certified that God is true. 34For He whom God has sent speaks the words of God, for God does not give the Spirit by measure. 35The Father loves the Son, and has given all things into His hand. 36He who believes in the Son has everlasting life; and he who does not believe the Son shall not see life, but the wrath of God abides on him."

SUCCESS

To what extent should Christ's followers today pursue success? John's declaration that "He must increase, but I must decrease" (John 3:30) seems to repudiate the idea of personal achievement, recognition, or material gain—common measures of success in our society. Indeed, John himself showed none of the outward trappings of a successful ministry.

So should believers avoid success as the world defines it? Can people be successful in their careers as well as in their spiritual lives, or are the two mutually exclusive? Some Christians say that success on the job creates credibility for them to talk about Christ with coworkers. Others, however, claim that they have no interest in being successful. But is that a genuine conviction, or are they merely avoiding the rough-and-tumble of a competitive marketplace? Would God prefer that His people be *failures* on the job, in society, or in life?

Questions like these barely scratch the surface of the complex, emotional issue of success. The people of Jesus' day were no less interested in prospering than we are, even if they defined success in slightly different terms. So it's not surprising that Scripture speaks to human ambition and achievement. It seems to affirm at least three important principles, as illustrated by John the Baptist:

(1) *Success is always measured by a set of standards established by some person or group.* Many people of John's day felt that they were assured of the blessing of God simply because they were descendants of Abraham. Their religious leaders aggressively promoted and reinforced that idea (Matt. 3:7–9; Luke 3:8; John 8:39). John challenged them to reconsider that way of thinking. What mattered, he said, was faith in Jesus. That was the ultimate criterion by which God would measure people's lives. Thus, unbelief would result in the ultimate failure— eternal death (John 3:36).

(2) *Why and how we pursue success is just as important as whether or not we achieve it.* John's listeners were ordinary people caught up in the everyday scramble to get ahead. But in their pursuit of gain they tended to ignore the needs of others and to take ethical shortcuts. John challenged them to make internal changes (that is, to repent) and to demonstrate those changes in their day-to-

day responsibilities through charity, honesty, and justice (Luke 3:8, 10–14).

John himself was able to carry out his ministry because he had the right perspective on the assignment that God had given him. He recognized that he was merely a forerunner to the Christ, not the Christ Himself (John 3:28–29). He knew that Jesus' ministry was going to grow and expand, slowly eliminating the need for John—hence his statement that "He must increase, but I must decrease."

(3) *Obtaining success always carries a cost.* John warned the people of God's judgment using a simple, well-known image: "Even now the ax is laid to the root of the trees. Therefore, every tree which does not bear fruit is cut down and thrown into the fire" (Luke 3:9). Just as a lumberjack would lay his ax at the foot of a tree while he decided which trees in a forest to cut, so God had sent John and Jesus as His final messengers before letting His judgment fall.

The people could choose what they wanted to do— whether to continue in their self-satisfied ways of unbelief, or whether to turn toward God in repentance and obedience. Either way, there would be a cost involved. Unfortunately, most of them chose to reject John's

continued

continued

message and later Jesus' message, with tragic results.

For John, the cost of faithfully proclaiming his message was imprisonment and, eventually, execution (Matt. 14:1–12). Yet he gained a treasure all out of proportion to the price of martyrdom—-the praise of Christ (Matt. 11:7–11).

So should believers pursue success? Judging from the experience of John the Baptist and the people who followed him, the issue seems to be not so much *whether* we should pursue it, but *how.* In light of John's message, it's worth considering three crucial questions:

- Who sets the standards by which I measure success?
- What are my motives and behavior in pursuing success?
- What price am I willing to pay to achieve success? ◆

 Luke 3:1–14

¹Now in the fifteenth year of the reign of Tiberius Caesar, Pontius Pilate being governor of Judea, Herod being tetrarch of Galilee, his brother Philip tetrarch of Iturea and the region of Trachonitis, and Lysanias tetrarch of Abilene, ²while Annas and Caiaphas were high priests, the word of God came to John the son of Zacharias in the wilderness. ³And he went into all the region around the Jordan, preaching a baptism of repentance for the remission of sins, ⁴as it is written in the book of the words of Isaiah the prophet, saying:

> "The voice of one crying in the
> wilderness:
> 'Prepare the way of the LORD;
> Make His paths straight.
> ⁵ Every valley shall be filled
> And every mountain and hill brought
> low;
> The crooked places shall be made
> straight
> And the rough ways smooth;
> ⁶ And all flesh shall see the salvation of
> God.' "

⁷Then he said to the multitudes that came out to be baptized by him, "Brood of vipers! Who warned you to flee from the wrath to come? ⁸Therefore bear fruits worthy of repentance, and do not begin to say to yourselves, 'We have Abraham as *our* father.' For I say to you that God is able to raise up children to Abraham from these stones. ⁹And even now the ax is laid to the root of the trees. Therefore every tree which does not bear good fruit is cut down and thrown into the fire."

¹⁰So the people asked him, saying, "What shall we do then?"

¹¹He answered and said to them, "He who has two tunics, let him give to him who has none; and he who has food, let him do likewise."

¹²Then tax collectors also came to be baptized, and said to him, "Teacher, what shall we do?"

¹³And he said to them, "Collect no more than what is appointed for you."

¹⁴Likewise the soldiers asked him, saying, "And what shall we do?"

So he said to them, "Do not intimidate anyone or accuse falsely, and be content with your wages."

How Do You Spell Success?

Place a check mark by the statements below that describe your ideas of success.

_____ Having a six-figure salary
_____ Having a large, expensive automobile
_____ Personal happiness
_____ Having friends
_____ Having maid service
_____ Being invited to exclusive parties

One of your coworkers is considering becoming a Christian, but he has one reservation: "It seems to me that in order to be a follower of Jesus, I can't be successful." How would you respond?

_____

_____

_____

◆ ◆ ◆ ◆ ◆ ◆ ◆ ◆ ◆

1. John the Baptist's idea of success was to point people to Jesus Christ, which is why he said, "He must increase, but I must decrease" (John 3:30). What is your primary motive for pursuing success? (For instance: so my children can enjoy a better lifestyle than I had as a child.)

_____

_____

_____

2. Success always has a price tag. What price are you paying in the following areas in order to be successful? Be as specific as possible.

My marriage: _____

_____

_____

My children: _____

_____

_____

My integrity: _____

_____

My spiritual life: _____

_____

My emotional health: _____

_____

My physical health: _____

_____

3a. Review your answers in question two, and place a check mark in front of each area in which you feel you are currently paying too much.

3b. For each area you checked, create a simple goal that will help you reduce the price.

_____

_____

_____

4. What prices are you absolutely unwilling to pay to achieve success?

_____

_____

_____

5. Skeptics might argue that the reward John the Baptist received—praise from Christ— seems a paltry prize compared to the price John paid. How would you answer such a statement?

_____

_____

_____

—— ✦ Use It or Lose It ✦ ——

Few people on earth could play a piano as well as Shannon. When he was barely able to reach the keyboard, he began to pick out notes that sounded surprisingly like good music—especially for a two-year-old. As Shannon grew older, his God-given gift seemed to grow with him. He never attended a formal music class; he was one of those naturally talented individuals for whom the music came effortlessly.

That may have been Shannon's downfall. Because the music came more easily for him than for a person with less ability, Shannon rarely applied himself to developing his talent. As an adult, he wrote some songs, played in some bands, and recorded a few albums as a studio musician, but he never achieved the level of success of which he was capable. Rather than risking failure in a larger arena, he was content to play for a local band.

When asked why he never attempted to do more with his music, Shannon's answer was disappointing. "I just do enough to make a few bucks here and there," he replied. "Just what is necessary and not inconvenient." ✦

✦ ✦ ✦ ✦ ✦ ✦ ✦ ✦ ✦

Do you recognize a bit of Shannon in you? Be careful! The comfortable become trapped by convenience and complacency. On the other hand, when you understand the true meaning of success, you want to be a good manager of the gifts God has given to you. Success may come easily or it may be something for which you have to sweat, suffer, and sacrifice. Success is not a matter of trying to make a great name for yourself; it is being faithful to God by using what He has given you to honor Him.

TRUE SUCCESS MEANS FAITHFULNESS

The story of the talents (Matt. 25:14–30) is about the kingdom of heaven (v. 14), but it offers an important lesson about success. God measures our success not by what we have, but by what we do with what we have—for all that we have is a gift from Him. We are really only managers to whom He has entrusted resources and responsibilities.

The key thing He looks for is *faithfulness* (vv. 21, 23), doing what we can to obey and honor Him with whatever He has given us. We may or may not be "successful" as our culture measures success, in terms of wealth, prestige, power, or fame. In the long run that hardly matters. What counts is whether we have faithfully served God with what He has entrusted to us. By all means we must avoid wasting our lives, the way the third servant wasted his talents, by failing to carry out our Master's business.

 Matthew 25:14–30

14"For *the kingdom of heaven* is like a man traveling to a far country, *who* called his own servants and delivered his goods to them. 15And to one he gave five talents, to another two, and to another one, to each according to his own ability; and immediately he went on a journey. 16Then he who had received the five talents went and traded with them, and made another five talents. 17And likewise he who *had received* two gained two more also. 18But he who had received one went and dug in the ground, and hid his lord's money. 19After a long time the lord of those servants came and settled accounts with them.

continued

continued

²⁰"So he who had received five talents came and brought five other talents, saying, 'Lord, you delivered to me five talents; look, I have gained five more talents besides them.' ²¹His lord said to him, 'Well *done*, good and faithful servant; you were faithful over a few things, I will make you ruler over many things. Enter into the joy of your lord.' ²²He also who had received two talents came and said, 'Lord, you delivered to me two talents; look, I have gained two more talents besides them.' ²³His lord said to him, 'Well *done*, good and faithful servant; you have been faithful over a few things, I will make you ruler over many things. Enter into the joy of your lord.'

²⁴"Then he who had received the one talent came and said, 'Lord, I knew you to be a hard man, reaping where you have not sown, and gathering where you have not scattered seed. ²⁵And I was afraid, and went and hid your talent in the ground. Look, *there* you have *what is* yours.'

²⁶"But his lord answered and said to him, 'You wicked and lazy servant, you knew that I reap where I have not sown, and gather where I have not scattered seed. ²⁷So you ought to have deposited my money with the bankers, and at my coming I would have received back my own with interest. ²⁸So take the talent from him, and give *it* to him who has ten talents.

²⁹"For to everyone who has, more will be given, and he will have abundance; but from him who does not have, even what he has will be taken away. ³⁰And cast the unprofitable servant into the outer darkness. There will be weeping and gnashing of teeth.'"

In the story of the talents, the master gave one fellow five talents, another two talents, and another one talent. A talent was worth about a thousand dollars.

The first two men invested their talents and when the master returned, they were given an appropriate reward. The fellow who had the least to lose was too timid to do anything with the talent that had been entrusted to him. He simply buried the talent, and when the master came back, he dug it out and gave it back to him. This man received a scathing rebuke, rather than a reward (vv. 26–28).

Though the talents in this story were measures of money, this principle governs the way you manage every gift and resource God has given to you. It's the old "use it or lose it" adage. Either use what the Lord has given to you for His glory, or it will be taken away from you and given to someone else. Whether you are extraordinarily gifted or not, always make the best of what God has given you. He will be pleased with you, and you will be pleased with yourself.

What talent have you been burying that God wants you to invest in His kingdom?

Faithfulness Is the Key

1a. In Matthew 25:15, notice that the master gave the men talents, "each according to his own ability." What effect should that have had on their fear of failure?

1b. What possible reasons could the men have for not faithfully using what was given to them?

_____

_____

_____

_____

_____

2. As a rule, the people who are happiest and most satisfied with their work are those whose work makes use of their God-given gifts, talents, and abilities. They love what they do and are doing what they love. Which statement reflects how you feel about your work?

_____ My work makes use of my talents.
_____ I feel that I am doing what I do best most of the time.
_____ Occasionally I am happy with what I am doing, but nothing about my work really excites me.
_____ I often feel out of place at work, like I don't belong there.
_____ I'm making a living, but I don't get a great sense of fulfillment from what I do at work.
_____ I feel I am wasting my time, talents, and abilities.

3. Based upon your own gifts, talents, and interests, if you could create your own job description, what would it be?

_____

_____

_____

_____

4. What are some practical things you can do to make better use of the talents God has given you?

_____

_____

_____

_____

◆ When the Price Isn't Right ◆

By all accounts, Bill Johnson was a hard worker. Some of Bill's coworkers worried that he was a workaholic. Bill was at work by six A.M. and was often still working as the clock struck midnight. Nobody ever criticized Bill's work habits . . . except his wife and kids. They rarely saw Bill for more than a few hours at a time, and even then his mind was preoccupied with his work.

Bill's wife viewed their disjointed lifestyle as part of the price they must pay for their comfortable home in the suburbs and for educating their children in the best schools. But she wasn't happy. The kids regarded their dad as an infrequent dinner guest. What time the family did spend together was always frenetic—hurry up; let's go; we're late. They were always rushing through life.

Spiritually, Bill and his family were running on empty. They still attended church, but it was mostly out of habit. Church was merely one more perfunctory appointment to be kept. When scheduling cuts had to be made, spiritual pursuits were the first to be compromised.

Bill had made it to the top in his profession. He received the respect of his peers and a substantial salary. People always called him Mr. Johnson when they saw him in town. Then one day, out of the blue, Bill walked into his boss's office . . . and quit.

"Why, Bill? Why?" his boss wanted to know. "Is it more money you want? You've got it. Name the figure and it's yours."

"No, that's not it," Bill replied. "I was sitting at my desk, looking out the window for a moment, when I began thinking, *A gold watch is not going to hug me when I get old.* Yes, I have achieved great success with our company, but so what? In the meantime, my kids are in trouble at school, my wife is ready to leave me, and I feel as though God is a million miles away. Before I squander away the relationships that are most precious to me, I'm going to change my priorities. I want to stop and smell the roses before the roses are all gone!" ◆

THE REAL BOTTOM LINE

Businesspeople commonly talk about the "bottom line," usually meaning the *financial* bottom line. In Luke 9:25 Christ challenges us to look at another bottom line—the final accounting each of us will give to God for how we have spent our lives.

Clearly one can be very successful from a human point of view and yet be finally lost.

Moreover, a careless Christian's works will be judged adversely. That can happen both actively and passively. Actively, we can sell out to the world's values by lying to a customer, cheating on a deal, or running over others to advance our position. Passively, we can drift away from God by leaving Him out of our work and lives, or perhaps by sacrificing our families in order to pursue wealth and status. Either way, the "bottom line" is clear: we will bring ourselves to ultimate loss.

 Luke 9:25

²⁵For what profit is it to a man if he gains the whole world, and is himself destroyed or lost?

1a. Maybe you haven't been trying to gain the entire world, but you have been pursuing some symbol of success. What is it?

_____

_____

1b. How much value will your goal have fifty years from now?

_____

_____

_____

2. What would you lose by pursuing goals that humans view as successful?

_____

_____

3. List some specific changes you want to make so your priorities meet God's "bottom line."

_____

_____

_____

_____

◆ What Good Is the Sabbath? ◆

Believe it or not, God never intended for you to work seven days a week. God Himself "took a break" on the seventh day following six days of vigorous creating. Scripture also reminds us that at times Jesus and His disciples got away from the clamoring crowds for periods of rest and prayer. You don't need to feel guilty when you take time out for rest, relaxation, and spiritual refreshment. That's why God created the Sabbath.

 Mark 6:30–32

[30]Then the apostles gathered to Jesus and told Him all things, both what they had done and what they had taught. [31]And He said to them, "Come aside by yourselves to a deserted place and rest a while." For there were many coming and going, and they did not even have time to eat. [32]So they departed to a deserted place in the boat by themselves.

WHY NOT REST A WHILE?

When the Twelve returned from their preaching tour (Mark 6:7, 12, 30), Jesus took them aside for a bit of rest and relaxation (v. 31). In doing so, He modeled a principle that many of us today could stand to practice more—the principle of rest.

Rest may seem to be the last thing we need, given industry's obsession with productivity and our culture's reputation as a "leisure society." But God wants us to adopt His values, not the values of our culture. One thing He values is leisure. He values work as well. But rest is something God Himself does (Gen. 2:2), which means that rest is good in and of itself. In fact, God actually commanded His people Israel to rest (Ex. 20:8–11).

Have you determined how much time you actually need to spend at work? Have you carefully considered how to balance your time and energy between workplace commitments and your family? Are you perhaps working too much, not because the job demands it, but because you won't trust God to supply your needs through a reasonable amount of work? Perhaps you need to take Jesus' advice: "Come aside . . . and rest a while."

Many sincere Christians fail to establish a Sabbath. They feel they are so busy they cannot afford to give up that time. Maybe you have heard yourself saying, "I can barely get everything done by working seven days a week! How would I possibly survive if I took off one day and set it apart as a day of rest and worship?"

Probably better. God did not create you to be a perpetual motion machine. He has set aside special times for His people to come together, to praise and worship Him, and to rest and refresh themselves. Healthy, balanced Christians recognize the value of setting apart at least one day each week as a time of rest, restoration, reflection, and worship.

1. List a few positive changes observing the Sabbath might bring about in your life. (For instance: By establishing a Sabbath, I could spend more quality time with my family.)

_____

_____

_____

_____

2. How would observing the Sabbath affect your attitude toward your work? (For example: It would temporarily allow me to escape the "rat race" and stimulate my creativity.)

_____

_____

_____

_____

3. How you keep the Sabbath is up to you. As a general guide for your activities (or in-activity!), ask yourself questions such as:
- Is this activity relaxing, restful, or restorative?
- Does this activity draw me closer to God or push me farther from Him?
- Will I be better or worse the rest of the week for having engaged in this activity on the Sabbath?

What are some fun, practical ways you might enjoy the Sabbath?

_____

_____

_____

_____

◆ ◆ ◆ ◆ ◆ ◆ ◆ ◆ ◆

So what is God's idea of success? Despite society's belief, it is not wealth, power, prestige, or fame. Granted, many Old Testament saints were extremely prosperous by their societies' standards. Nevertheless, it would be a broad generalization to assume that faith in God and obedience to His Word automatically bring worldly success.

The Bible promises a reward to believers who gauge their success or failure by God's standards and seek to please Him. By following God's standards, you may or may not be rewarded in this life. However, you certainly will be rewarded in heaven.

Can a Christian be successful in this world? Certainly! But where the world's idea of success clashes with God's true success, the believer must be ready to willingly place everything in the hands of Christ. Furthermore, every believer has a responsibility to use the gifts, talents, and resources from God in a way that pleases Him.

Most of us need help in that area, which is why God's Word instructs us to be openly accountable to each other. Scripture teaches that believers have a mutual obligation to help keep one another on the right track in life. In other words, your business really is your fellow believer's business.

You're Not the Lone Ranger

Are you going to let him talk to you that way?" Pete hissed into Jack's ear.

"It's okay. Take it easy," Jack replied. "You wanted to come to this lunch meeting to see what our accountability group is all about, didn't you?"

"Yes, but I didn't think it was going to be a return to the days of the Inquisition!"

"Calm down, I have given these guys permission to ask me tough questions about my life, and they expect me to do the same for them. I'd be disappointed if they didn't care enough to dig into some sensitive areas. Just sit back and listen."

"Okay, but I think you're nuts. This is a free country, you know. You don't have to tell anybody anything about your personal life."

Jack laughed and patted Pete on the back as the two men returned to the restaurant table, where Art and Chuck were waiting for them. The three men in the accountability group were employed by the same company. Once a week during their lunch hour they got together to question each other about how well they were maintaining their rela-tionships with God, their families, and their coworkers.

This week the guys had consented to allow Pete to observe how the group functioned. Pete appreciated their openness, but was surprised at the men's bluntness. The group's intent was not to intrude in somebody else's business, nor was it to condemn anyone. They met to encourage each other.

"Let's see, where were we?" Art asked.

"We were discussing Jack's use of time at work," Chuck offered.

"Yes, that's right," said Jack. "It seems like lately I've been focusing too much time on the volunteer work I am doing. Sometimes, the only time I can reach people is when I call them during the day.

"I try not to take too much time away from my work to make the calls, but before I know it, I've spent two hours making these calls!

"Then I tell myself I'll take work home at night to make up for the lost time, but by the time I play with the kids, eat dinner, and talk with my wife, it's time for bed. There just aren't enough hours during the day."

"But, Jack," Art spoke softly, "don't you think you are cheating your boss and your company by doing volunteer work when you should be doing your job?"

Chuck chimed in sympathetically, "I used to do a lot of volunteer work. I started out doing a few things here and there. Next thing I knew, I was asked to do more and more . . . I couldn't say no."

"That's exactly what happened to me," Jack replied. "What did you do?"

"I finally realized that I had to budget my time. I still do volunteer work, but I only do what I have time to do at night or on the weekends. Maybe you could do the same."

Jack knew Chuck was right. "Maybe I could contact the people in charge of the volunteers and ask them to find someone to take over some of my responsibilities."

"That's a great idea!" exclaimed Art. "You'll feel much better once you have regained balance in your life."

"Thanks, guys," Jack said. "I sure am glad I mentioned this to you."

Accountability. For many of us it is the missing ingredient in our spiritual lives. After all, most of us don't like someone else's looking over our shoulders and keeping track of how we're doing. But God never intended for you to function as a "Spiritual Lone Ranger." Most of us need someone who loves us enough to look us in the eyes and say, "I don't think that would be a wise move to make." There is strength and security in knowing that someone who loves you is watching out for you and is willing to tell you the truth when necessary, even if it hurts sometimes.

ACCOUNTABILITY

The discipline of a Corinthian believer (2 Cor. 2:6) points to one of the important functions of the body of Christ—to hold its members accountable for how they conduct their lives. In the case mentioned here, the censure of the church caused the offender to repent and change his ways, restoring his spiritual life and bringing joy to the church.

Accountability is easy to talk about but difficult to practice. No one likes to be judged by others. In modern society it's especially easy to feel that one's personal life is no one else's business. But a study of Scripture reveals a number of important principles about accountability:

(1) As believers, we are accountable not only for our actions, but also for our attitudes. In the performance-oriented work world, evaluations tend to measure results alone—higher sales, greater cost control, more clients served. Everything is quantitative. But God is interested in our innermost heart. He looks at the quality of our character. As God told Samuel, "The Lord does not see as man sees; for man looks at the outward appearance, but the Lord looks at the heart" (1 Sam. 16:7).

(2) Accountability depends on trust. To hold ourselves accountable to others is to trust their judgment and to believe that they are committed to the same truths and values that we are. It also helps if we can sense that they have our best interests at heart. That's why Paul pleaded with the Corinthians to forsake their divisions and "be perfectly joined together in the same mind and in the same judgment" (1 Cor. 1:10). Without that unity, they would never submit to each other.

(3) Accountability is directly related to the principle of submission. Every person must struggle with the natural tendency toward rebellion against God. Accountability involves allowing others to enter into that struggle with us. But that means that sometimes we must defer to the judgment or counsel of another, especially when they challenge us with clear-cut Scriptural truth or the wisdom of personal experience. Paul told the Ephesians that part of living in the will of the Lord involves "submitting to one another in the fear of God" (Eph. 5:21).

It's not surprising that participation in the body of Christ would involve accountability, because all of us experience accountability in many other areas of life. For example, the government holds us accountable for obeying the law and paying taxes. Likewise, government officials are accountable to the public for their decisions. Employees are accountable to the boss for their work. Likewise, corporate officers are accountable to stockholders for quarterly financial results. In short, accountability touches us at home, at work, at church, and even at play.

But our attitudes toward accountability in general ultimately reflect our attitude toward accountability to God. If we are rebellious toward the One who created us and loves us most, how able will we be to submit to others? ◆

2 Corinthians 2:5–11

⁵But if anyone has caused grief, he has not grieved me, but all of you to some extent—not to be too severe. ⁶This punishment which *was inflicted* by the majority is sufficient for such a man, ⁷so that, on the contrary, you *ought* rather to forgive and comfort *him*, lest perhaps such a one be swallowed up with too much sorrow. ⁸Therefore I urge you to reaffirm *your* love to him. ⁹For to this end I also wrote, that I might put you to the test, whether you are obedient in all things. ¹⁰Now whom you forgive anything, I also *forgive*. For if indeed I have forgiven anything, I have forgiven that one for your sakes in the presence of Christ, ¹¹lest Satan should take advantage of us; for we are not ignorant of his devices.

1. In 2 Corinthians 2:5–11, Scripture teaches that it is the church's responsibility to enforce biblical standards among its members, and that individual members are to hold one another accountable. What is the ultimate goal of church discipline?

_____

_____

_____

2. Paul implies that Satan can somehow take advantage of us through a lack of church discipline (2:11). List some ways you think Satan might be able to do this.

_____

_____

_____

3a. What are some reasons you may be reluctant to enter into an accountability relationship with another believer?

_____

_____

_____

3b. What do you see as the value of having such an accountability partner or group?

_____

_____

_____

—◆ Doing the Right Thing ◆—

George carefully held the check in his hands. He allowed his fingertips to trace the amount written on the check: five thousand dollars. George needed the money desperately, but he knew it didn't belong to him. A customer had overpaid him, and now George was wondering what he should do about it. He could cash the check and the customer would never be suspicious. After all,

the customer thought he actually owed the extra money.

Should he return the check? If he did that, what would happen to the customer's employee who had written the check? If George returned it, the employee might be punished or possibly terminated. Maybe everyone would be better off if George just kept his mouth shut and cashed the check. George

bounced the possibilities back and forth in his thoughts.

He finally concluded that he had only one choice. He placed the check in an envelope with a brief letter of explanation, and sent it back to the customer. As he dropped the envelope in the mailbox, he thought, *Well, I may have five thousand dollars less in the bank, but at least I can sleep tonight with a clear conscience.* ◆

◆ ◆ ◆ ◆ ◆ ◆ ◆ ◆ ◆

Doing the Christlike thing in the workplace doesn't always bring about favorable results. Sometimes doing the right thing costs you! But it will be worth it because ultimately we are accountable to God. He is the One who will review how your actions and attitudes impacted people, property, and profitability.

PEOPLE, PROPERTY, AND PROFITABILITY

The gospel can produce radical changes as it affects people, property, and profitability. Consider three instructive examples from Acts:

Simon "the Great" (Acts 8:9–13, 18–24)

- *A sorcerer with a large following.*
- *The gospel threatened his profitable business by demonstrating a greater power.*
- *Hoping to expand his repertoire, he offered to buy the apostles' power.*
- *Rebuked by the apostles, who called him to true repentance.*

The Slave Girl at Philippi (Acts 16:16–40)

- *Paul's gospel freed a fortune-teller from her occult bondage.*
- *Owned by a syndicate of investors, she had powers that earned them good money.*

continued

continued

- *Realizing their loss, they seized Paul and Silas and hauled them before the authorities.*
- *Punishment: beatings and jail.*
- *But lockup only led to further conversions.*
- *Morning brought embarrassment to the city as officials learned of the travelers' Roman citizenship.*

The Silversmiths at Ephesus (Acts 19:1–41)

- *Paul lectured daily in the school of Tyrannus, resulting in many conversions.*
- *Sales of silver statues of Diana (the Greek goddess of fertility) fell off, triggering an emergency "Chamber of Commerce" meeting.*
- *Artisans complained that Paul's gospel had reduced trade, ruined their reputations, and impugned their goddess.*
- *A riot was incited and Paul's associates were dragged before a lynch mob.*
- *The city clerk eventually restored peace and Paul quietly went on his way.*

Good Ethics—Not Always Good Business

Christlike values do not necessarily produce financial gain in the marketplace. Sometimes they produce just the opposite. Scripture has no argument with making a profit except when it compromises people or the truth. At that point the gospel raises questions that any responsible believer must face. For example, a contract goes unsigned because a Christian refuses to offer money under the table. A sale is lost because a Christian refuses to lie to a customer. A promotion slips by because a Christian sets limits on the intrusion of work into his or her family and personal life.

Make no mistake, many people are receptive toward Christian principles at home and church, and even on the job—as long as such principles cost nothing. But the test of Christian commitment often lies in what one is willing to sacrifice.

What have your Christian convictions cost you? If nothing, are you making tradeoffs that you can't afford to make? Do you sometimes value possessions or power more than people? ◆

 Acts 16:16–24

[16]Now it happened, as we went to prayer, that a certain slave girl possessed with a spirit of divination met us, who brought her masters much profit by fortune-telling. [17]This girl followed Paul and us, and cried out, saying, "These men are the servants of the Most High God, who proclaim to us the way of salvation." [18]And this she did for many days.

But Paul, greatly annoyed, turned and said to the spirit, "I command you in the name of Jesus Christ to come out of her." And he came out that very hour. [19]But when her masters saw that their hope of profit was gone, they seized Paul and Silas and dragged *them* into the marketplace to the authorities.

[20]And they brought them to the magistrates, and said, "These men, being Jews, exceedingly trouble our city; [21]and they teach customs which are not lawful for us, being Romans, to receive or observe." [22]Then the multitude rose up together against them; and the magistrates tore off their clothes and commanded *them* to be beaten with rods. [23]And when they had laid many stripes on them, they threw *them* into prison, commanding the jailer to keep them securely. [24]Having received such a charge, he put them into the inner prison and fastened their feet in the stocks.

---

1. Which phrase best describes your attitudes and actions in regard to people, property, and profitability?

    _____ I love people and use things.
    _____ I use people and love things.

2. What relationship do you see between financial profitability and a willingness to use or deceive people in order to get ahead?

_____

_____

_____

_____

3. In Acts 16:17–18, why do you think Paul was annoyed with the slave girl's actions and words?

_____

_____

_____

_____

4. The slave girl's masters were exploiting her for their own profits. List some contemporary examples in which you believe employers are exploiting their employees. (Your examples do not have to be exclusive to your workplace.)

_____

_____

_____

_____

5. Paul and Silas were stripped of their clothes, beaten with rods, and thrown into prison . . . all for helping to deliver the slave girl from her bondage. Briefly describe a time when you did the right thing in your workplace, but were treated wrongly as a result.

_____

_____

_____

_____

◆ God Owns My Business ◆

Being an accountable believer in the workplace concerns more than how faithful you are in your spiritual disciplines and how you treat other people and property. It concerns your attitude toward material possessions, too. It reaches to the matter of who is really in charge of your life. The couple in the following story realized who is in charge.

◆ ◆ ◆ ◆ ◆ ◆ ◆ ◆ ◆

Stanley Tam and his wife Juanita owned a fledgling business that they ran out of a trailer. Before the couple married, Stanley had nearly given up on the company. But one day, while he was driving along the highway near Columbus, Ohio, Stanley sensed that God was speaking to him about his business. He realized that God was asking him to turn the business over to Him, so Stanley obeyed. He promised God that he would honor Him through the company.

Shortly after Stanley and Juanita married, Stanley began to understand how he should turn his business over to God. He shared his conviction with Juanita and she quickly agreed. Their plan was to make God their senior partner and a fifty-one percent owner of their company. Fifty-one percent of all profits would be given away to Christian ministries.

Once the Tams found a lawyer willing to draw up the corporate papers naming God as senior partner—no small feat in itself—they established the Stanita Foundation. God began to bless their business beyond their expectations. They gave so much money away that the Internal Revenue Service audited their books for ten consecutive years! The IRS could not understand how the Tams could make a better profit on only forty-nine percent of the company than most people do by owning one hundred percent of a business.

Then, while Stanley and Juanita were taking part in a missions trip to Medellin, Colombia, the couple faced an even greater challenge. Stanley sensed the Lord was speaking to him again, and the instructions were clear. God wanted the Tams to turn their entire business over to Him—not ten percent, not fifty-one percent, but one hundred percent of the two companies the Tams now owned. Stanley and Juanita Tam obeyed God and became employees of their own company, relinquishing their forty-nine percent ownership to God. And God continued to prosper His company and His employees. When anyone asked Stanley the secret to his success, Stanley's answer was simple: "God owns my business." ◆

◆ ◆ ◆ ◆ ◆ ◆ ◆ ◆ ◆

Maybe you don't own a business that you could give God. But the matter of who is in charge of what you do have is just as important for you as it was for Stanley and Juanita Tam. How do you regard your possessions? Are they yours or are they merely on loan from God?

OWNERS OR TENANTS?

Are we the owners of possessions like money, houses, land, cars, clothing, TV sets, and so forth? Our culture tells us that we are. In fact, many messages tell us that significance is determined by how much we own and how much what we own is worth. But the parable of the vineyard owner (Luke 20:9–19)

continued

continued

challenges that way of looking at things. Jesus tells of tenants or workers who scheme to steal a vineyard from its owner rather than return its produce to him. They value the land, the trees, and the fruit more than people—they beat the owner's representatives (vv. 10–12)—and even more than life itself—they kill the owner's own son (vv. 14–15).

In the same way, the community leaders among Jesus' listeners harbored the same desire to kill Him (v. 19). At that point, however, they were prevented from acting by the rest of the people. But eventually they would have their way. Just as their forebears had rejected the prophets that God had sent, so they would now reject God's own Son in a futile effort to keep the nation under their control. But they would only succeed in bringing down God's judgment.

This parable challenges us to consider what God has entrusted to our care, and what He expects from us. No matter what He has given us, we are like tenants; the true Owner of all things is the Creator God. He has loaned us our lives, our families, our skills, and all our resources. He calls us to manage those gifts in a way that honors Him.

That means that we must resist getting so tied to our possessions and the accumulation of more possessions that we are tempted to resort to evil or even violence to keep them. We must hold things with the attitude of tenants, keeping in mind who really owns them—God who loaned them to us for His glory and the service of others. ◆

♦ ♦ ♦ ♦ ♦ ♦ ♦ ♦ ♦

 Luke 20:9–19

⁹Then He began to tell the people this parable: "A certain man planted a vineyard, leased it to vinedressers, and went into a far country for a long time. ¹⁰Now at vintage-time he sent a servant to the vinedressers, that they might give him some of the fruit of the vineyard. But the vinedressers beat him and sent *him* away empty-handed. ¹¹Again he sent another servant; and they beat him also, treated *him* shamefully, and sent *him* away empty-handed. ¹²And again he sent a third; and they wounded him also and cast *him* out.

¹³"Then the owner of the vineyard said, 'What shall I do? I will send my beloved son. Probably they will respect *him* when they see him.' ¹⁴But when the vinedressers saw him, they reasoned among themselves, saying, 'This is the heir. Come, let us kill him, that the inheritance may be ours.' ¹⁵So they cast him out of the vineyard and killed him. Therefore what will the owner of the vineyard do to them? ¹⁶He will come and destroy those vinedressers and give the vineyard to others."

And when they heard *it* they said, "Certainly not!"

¹⁷Then He looked at them and said, "What then is this that is written:

'The stone which the builders rejected
Has become the chief cornerstone' ?

¹⁸Whoever falls on that stone will be broken; but on whomever it falls, it will grind him to powder."

¹⁹And the chief priests and the scribes that very hour sought to lay hands on Him, but they feared the people—for they knew He had spoken this parable against them.

1. It's one thing to say that we want God to be in charge of all our possessions; it's quite another to actually live by that principle. Thinking back over the past few weeks, which of the "vineyards" below did you use for your own selfishness and which were used for God's glory? Mark "M" (My own selfishness) or "G" (God's glory) for each.

_____ The house
_____ The car
_____ The telephone
_____ The television
_____ The food
_____ The bank accounts
_____ The computer or other office equipment
_____ The golf clubs

2a. Scan through the parable of the vineyard owner again (Luke 20:9–19) and identify each of the characters about whom Jesus was really addressing the story.

The owner of the vineyard: _____

The vinedressers (the tenants): _____

The servants: _____

The son: _____

The others to whom the vineyard is given: _____

2b. What was the response of the group toward whom Jesus directed this parable (20:19)?

_____

_____

_____

_____

3. Imagine that all your possessions are borrowed and you will have to return them soon. When you return them, you will have to tell the owner how the items were used. What would you say?

_____

_____

_____

_____

◆ Time Is Not on Your Side ◆

Perhaps the most difficult area of accountability is our time. Despite expensive time management seminars, computerized schedules, and beautiful organizers (most of which remain unused), we are painfully aware that time slips by much too quickly. Everything takes longer than we anticipated, and we never seem to get done nearly as much as we had hoped.

We all know that we won't be here forever. But does this knowledge inspire us to use our time wisely? In many cases it does not. If anything, this thought encourages us to work faster, harder, and longer. It's as if we are saying to ourselves, I must accomplish all my goals, so get out of my way; I'm in a hurry!

Wait a minute! If God intends for you to do something, doesn't it make sense to believe that He will provide you the time to do it? Is it God's priority list that you are following, or do you have your calendar crammed so full of nonessentials that God Himself has trouble squeezing into your schedule?

Maybe that is why God occasionally interrupts our plans. He wants to remind us of what is really important in life.

HOLY INTERRUPTIONS

How full is your schedule? Is it booked so tightly that only an act of God seems able to force an adjustment?

Jesus certainly had a demanding task with lots of responsibility. God sent Him to earth to gain salvation for all and to launch the church—and gave Him little more than three years to do it! Yet somehow Jesus' value system allowed for what we would call interruptions. People barged into His presence, even when His associates tried to prevent them.

Such was the case for a blind beggar by a roadside near Jericho (Luke 18:35–38). The man called out to Jesus as He and His leadership team were on their way to major events in Jerusalem. Then as now, well-traveled roads were cluttered with such inconveniences. Some tried to ignore the beggar, or at least keep him away. But amazingly, Jesus stopped and met the man's needs.

It's interesting that Jesus' very next encounter, with a known government crook, was also an interruption (Luke 19:1–10). Yet again, Jesus set aside His travel plans and turned aside to Zacchaeus' home to talk with him and meet his family and friends.

Do you have room for others in your life, especially the "little people" such as your children, an entry-level employee, a visitor to your church, or someone poor? When Jesus took time to serve a forgotten castaway, it caused everyone nearby to give praise to God (Luke 18:43). Watch out for God's holy interruptions!

 Luke 18:35–43

³⁵Then it happened, as He was coming near Jericho, that a certain blind man sat by the road begging. ³⁶And hearing a multitude passing by, he asked what it meant. ³⁷So they told him that Jesus of Nazareth was passing by. ³⁸And he cried out, saying, "Jesus, Son of David, have mercy on me!"

³⁹Then those who went before warned him that he should be quiet; but he cried out all the more, "Son of David, have mercy on me!"

continued

> *continued*
> ⁴⁰So Jesus stood still and commanded him to be brought to Him. And when he had come near, He asked him, ⁴¹saying, "What do you want Me to do for you?"
>
> He said, "Lord, that I may receive my sight."
>
> ⁴²Then Jesus said to him, "Receive your sight; your faith has made you well." ⁴³And immediately he received his sight, and followed Him, glorifying God. And all the people, when they saw *it*, gave praise to God.

1. When God interrupts your schedule, how do you usually respond?

_____ Oh, no! Not again.
_____ What a great opportunity!
_____ I can't get anything done around here.
_____ Lord, are You trying to get my attention?

2. Check your answers for the following questions:
Are you busier than Jesus was while He was here on earth?

_____ yes   _____ no

Is your work more important than His was?

_____ yes   _____ no

Are you on a tighter schedule than Jesus was?

_____ yes   _____ no

Jesus interrupted His own plans to meet the needs of other people, do you?

_____ yes   _____ no

Jesus found time to pray, do you?

_____ yes   _____ no

3a. In the account of the blind beggar who called out to Jesus from along the roadside (Luke 18:35–43), Jesus was on His way to Jerusalem to suffer and die on a cross. As far as we know, Jesus never passed this way again. Had the man not called out to Jesus that day, and had Jesus not taken time to minister to him that day, the man would have spent the rest of his life in blindness and poverty. Describe a "once in a lifetime opportunity" that God has placed in your path.

_____

_____

_____

_____

3b. In regard to that situation I felt _____

_____

_____

3c. If I ever have a similar opportunity, I will _____

_____

_____

4. Why do you suppose the people around Jesus tried to quiet the blind beggar and keep him away from Jesus?

_____

_____

_____

◆ ◆ ◆ ◆ ◆ ◆ ◆ ◆ ◆

The Bible clearly establishes the fact that Christians must be accountable for our actions and attitudes, as well as for the possessions, wealth, and time that God grants us. Most of the accountability issues boil down to one central question: *What are you doing with what God has given to you?* The corollary to that essential question is: *How can I best glorify God with what He has given to me?*

Perhaps no area of accountability is more scrutinized, investigated, and examined than the area of your money. Questions about the use and misuse of money abound. How do you get it? Where does it all go? How can you keep more of it? What are the dangers of having it (or not having it)? How can I better use what money I have? Get out your checkbook; in the next chapter, we're going to discover the balance between dollars and sense.

MONEY, MONEY, AND MORE MONEY!

Money talks—but what is it saying to you? Better still, what does it say about *you*? Place a check mark in front of the statements below that best reflect your attitude toward your possessions, your priorities, and your paycheck.

_____ I owe, I owe, so off to work I go.

_____ I am happy with my current pay.

_____ I want it all, and I want it now.

_____ If my family and I have a comfortable life, that's all that matters to me.

_____ Money can't buy me happiness, but maybe I can rent it for a while.

If you had enough money to live comfortably for the rest of your life, what work would you want to do, if any?

_____

_____

_____

_____

◆ ◆ ◆ ◆ ◆ ◆ ◆ ◆ ◆

Few things impact our lives as much as the "almighty dollar." For most of us it deter-mines where we live, where we work, what we do with our time, where (or if) we go on vacation, what we eat, what kind of clothes we wear, what type of car we drive, and where and when we will re-tire.

Money is much more than a means of exchange. In many ways, your money is you. How you make your money and how you spend or save it are some of the clearest indi-cators in your life regarding your priorities and commit-ments.

For most people, money means power. Those who have money, have clout. The person who controls the purse strings calls the shots. For some people, money means security. For others it is a means of control. Sometimes it signifies independence. Of-ten it is viewed as a source of status or self-esteem. When you realize the emotional sig-nificance money holds for most people, it is easy to un-derstand how people become trapped.

Some Christians distort biblical passages concerning money in an attempt to justify their desires. Others shun money for themselves and look suspiciously at anyone who is financially prosperous. Yet, in our society we all need some amount of money to survive. How can a Christian keep a proper attitude toward money? The following article offers some practical sugges-tions.

CHRISTIANS AND MONEY

Paul ridicules the idea that God is in the business of dispensing material gain in exchange for spiritual cooperation (1 Tim. 6:5). That launches him into a discussion of money that modern believers do well to study carefully, given the emphasis on money in our culture. He speaks to three categories of people: those who want to get rich (vv. 6–10), those who want to honor God (vv. 11–16), and those who are rich and want to honor God (vv. 17–19).

Contentment versus Covetousness (vv. 6–10)

Paul warns us strongly against "the love of money" (v. 10). But let's be sure we interpret his words correctly. He does not say that money itself is evil (nor does any other Scripture). Neither does he say that money is *the* fundamental root of evil, or that money lies at the root of *every* evil. Rather, the *love* of money (something inside people, not money itself) can be *a* root (but not the only root) of all *kinds* of evil (but not of all evil).

But don't let those qualifications soften the blow: people who love money are vulnerable to all kinds of evil, the worst of which, Paul points out, is straying from the faith.

Given that danger, believers should by all means avoid greed. Jesus gave a direct, unequivocal command to that effect. He didn't tell us to guard against it in others, but in ourselves.

Paul offers the alternative to greed, or covetousness, as contentment (vv. 6–8). However, his description of contentment—food and clothing—sounds incredibly spartan in our own culture that extols self-made millionaires and entertains itself by paying video visits to those who live in opulent, even decadent, lifestyles. Are believers required to take vows of poverty like Franciscan monks?

No, but Paul does remind us in this passage what poverty really is: lack of food, clothing, and shelter adequate for survival where one lives. If we have these, we ought to be content. If not, then we are truly destitute and dependent on the charity of others for survival. The biblical concept of poverty is not merely having less than the average income, or some percentage of it, in one's society, as contemporary sociologists and economists tend to define it.

continued

continued

Can Paul be serious? Is it really possible to be content, at least in our society, with merely the basics—food, clothing, and shelter? Paul should know. He experienced firsthand the wealth and privileges of prominence in the Jewish community and of Roman citizenship. Yet he also suffered extraordinary hardships in his work. Through it all he learned a secret that helped him maintain contentment. What was it?

A Charge to Timothy (vv. 11–16)

Paul's example was especially important to Timothy, his protégé in the faith. He challenges the young pastor to pursue a lifestyle that values character over cash (1 Tim. 6:11). The words are addressed to Timothy, but they apply to anyone who wants to honor God in life. Timothy needed to watch out for greed just like any other believer.

Paul was especially on the lookout for greed. Interestingly, one of his main strategies for avoiding it was to earn his own living as a tentmaker, rather than live off the generosity of others.

Commands for Rich Christians (vv. 17–19)

Apparently there were wealthy believers in Timothy's church at Ephesus. The city was ex-traordinarily prosperous. In fact, its tourist trade brought in so much revenue that the town leaders opened the first world bank. Paul had penetrated this vibrant economic life with the gospel, winning many converts. No doubt some of the rich Christians he addresses here brought their money with them into the faith—just like many in the modern church.

The question, then, especially in light of the teaching in 1 Timothy 6:6–10, is, what should people with money do if they want to honor God? Paul says they should start by examining their attitudes. Money has incredible power to create feelings of pride, superiority, and self-sufficiency (v. 17). So people of means have to learn to look beyond their money to God, the ultimate source of wealth.

But attitude is only half the battle. Sooner or later rich Christians need to take conscious, decisive action with their wealth. They need to put it into play serving God and others (v. 18).

What About You?

What is your deepest desire? Is it to be rich rather than righteous? If so, beware! Longing for wealth leads to many dangers—even to death. God wants you to grasp something far more permanent and satisfying—eternal life (vv. 12, 18). ◆

 1 Timothy 6:6–19

⁶Now godliness with contentment is great gain. ⁷For we brought nothing into *this* world, *and it is* certain we can carry nothing out. ⁸And having food and clothing, with these we shall be content. ⁹But those who desire to be rich fall into temptation and a snare, and *into* many foolish and harmful lusts which drown men in destruction and perdition. ¹⁰For the love of money is a root of all *kinds of* evil, for which some have strayed from the faith in their greediness, and pierced themselves through with many sorrows.

¹¹But you, O man of God, flee these things and pursue righteousness, godliness, faith, love, patience, gentleness. ¹²Fight the good fight of faith, lay hold on eternal life, to which you were also called and have confessed the good confession in the presence of many witnesses. ¹³I urge you in the sight of God who gives life to all things, and *before* Christ Jesus who witnessed the good confession before Pontius Pilate, ¹⁴that you keep *this* commandment without spot, blameless until our

continued

> *continued*
> Lord Jesus Christ's appearing, ¹⁵which He will manifest in His own time, *He who is* the blessed and only Potentate, the King of kings and Lord of lords, ¹⁶who alone has immortality, dwelling in unapproachable light, whom no man has seen or can see, to whom *be* honor and everlasting power. Amen.
>
> ¹⁷Command those who are rich in this present age not to be haughty, nor to trust in uncertain riches but in the living God, who gives us richly all things to enjoy. ¹⁸*Let them* do good, that they be rich in good works, ready to give, willing to share, ¹⁹storing up for themselves a good foundation for the time to come, that they may lay hold on eternal life.

1a. Notice Paul's prescription for true riches in 6:6. Fill in the essential ingredients in the formula below.

_____ + _____ = great gain

1b. In your opinion, what constitutes the wealth that Paul is speaking of here? (For instance: By feeling inner peace with God, I will be wealthy.)

_____

_____

2. According to verses 9–10, what are some of the most serious dangers facing a person who is lured by the love of money?

_____

_____

3a. List some of the things that you regard as real needs in your life right now. (For instance: I must have medicine for my child's chronic illness.)

_____

_____

3b. What are some ways God might meet those needs?

_____

_____

4. In Paul's instructions to Timothy (vv. 11–16), the apostle implies that contentment can be learned. According to this passage, list some things you can do to help you develop contentment.

_____

_____

◆ God Wants You to Be Rich! ◆

It's true! God does want you to be rich; but the wealth He has in mind for you may not be measurable in dollars and cents. We live in a materialistic society, and unfortunately the world's values have seeped into our collective Christian psyche. In some circles, it is even implied that if you are not being blessed financially and materially, then something must be wrong with you spiritually. In our efforts to show how "successful" we are, we forget that we serve Someone who didn't even have a place to call home during His earthly ministry.

This idea has come to be known as "prosperity theology." It is often promoted by magnetic personalities who, consciously or unconsciously, build their cases upon their interpretation of selected Scripture passages. Presented outside the context, these isolated passages are used to imply a convenient truth at best, and in the worst cases, a distorted doctrine of deception. Material blessings are used as motivation to follow Jesus, and financial wealth and overall prosperity are purported to be part of the "normal" Christian lifestyle.

Does it sound too good to be true? It is. In the following article, you will discover some reasons why prosperity theology is dangerously deceptive.

THE DANGERS OF PROSPERITY THEOLOGY

Susan is a sales representative. She can make a big sale, but only if she mildly deceives the customer. She decides to tell the truth and she loses the sale. Should she expect God to honor her integrity by helping her make an even bigger sale in the future?

A contractor is deciding whether to award a job to Allen's firm or to another company. Allen really needs the business. So he prays at length that he will get the contract, and asks others to pray, too. Should he anticipate that God will somehow make the contractor award him the job? If not, should he expect God to arrange for other work to come along soon?

John and Joan are reviewing their finances. John has recently received a small bonus from his company, and they're wondering what to do with it. They finally decide to give ten percent of it to their church, and another ten percent to a mission. Can they expect God to bring them more money as a result?

Does God reward godliness with material blessing? Not ac-cording to 1 Timothy 6:5. In fact, Paul describes those who teach that as being "destitute of the truth." They are guilty of fostering a "prosperity theology." That's a dangerous view:

It encourages perverted motives. God wants us to seek Him for His own sake, not for a "payoff" of physical well-being or financial gain. The reward of loving obedience is a closer relationship to God (John 14:15–18, 21–23). He also wants us to be content with what He provides us, not greedy for more (v. 6).

It misinterprets God's deepest concerns for us. If God wants us to have abundant material benefits, if He sees that they would

continued

continued

be in our best interest, then we can trust Him to supply them. Otherwise, such "blessings" would be harmful. God loves us too much to destroy us with what we don't need or can't handle.

It misrepresents God's promises in Scripture. The Old Testament offers plenty of promises about material prosperity and blessing. But for the most part, those benefits were offered to the nation of Israel, not to individual believers.

Furthermore, God's promises are always offered to those who truly love Him, seek His will, and obey Him from a pure heart. The Lord Himself is always the end to be sought; material benefits are never an end in themselves.

A final note: God has established certain "moral laws" that benefit anyone who adheres to them. (The Proverbs are filled with prudent advice that rewards those who keep them.) For example, paying taxes avoids the trouble, fines, prison terms, and public censure associated with nonpayment. In this sense it "pays" to obey the law. But we shouldn't expect special blessing for doing what God wants us to do anyway (Luke 17:7–10). ◆

---

 1 Timothy 6:3–6

³If anyone teaches otherwise and does not consent to wholesome words, *even* the words of our Lord Jesus Christ, and to the doctrine which accords with godliness, ⁴he is proud, knowing nothing, but is obsessed with disputes and arguments over words, from which come envy, strife, reviling, evil suspicions, ⁵useless wranglings of men of corrupt minds and destitute of the truth, who suppose that godliness is a *means of* gain. From such withdraw yourself.

⁶Now godliness with contentment is great gain.

How Can It Be Wrong When It Sounds So Right?

Wait a minute! Didn't Jesus teach us to give in order to receive? He seems to imply that as we give to others, something will be given to us. Jesus said, "Give, and it will be given to you: good measure, pressed down, shaken together, and running over will be put into your bosom. For with the same measure that you use, it will be measured back to you" (Luke 6:38). And didn't the apostle Paul remind us, "He who sows sparingly will also reap sparingly, and he who sows bountifully will also reap bountifully" (2 Cor. 9:6)?

Jesus did talk about treasures for every person who chooses to follow Him, but those treasures are in heaven. In regard to discipleship, Jesus discussed costs more than He did profits. And while Paul did encourage believers to give liberally, he also notes that the motive for giving must be just.

◆ ◆ ◆ ◆ ◆ ◆ ◆ ◆ ◆

1. God does promise to supply everything you need, and His Word promises that you will reap according to how you sow. Yet prosperity theology often perverts God's meaning. Where is the balance? What factors make the difference?

2. Many prosperity teachers place little emphasis upon ministering to impoverished ghettos or to Third World countries. Why do you suppose they neglect these groups?

_____

_____

3. Gaining godliness is a greater goal than pursuing material prosperity, but your godliness is not validated by wealth nor poverty. How will you know if you are gaining or losing with God?

_____

_____

◆ The Price Is Wrong! ◆

The Bible has much to say about money. It speaks of spending, saving, and investing money. Scripture also states plainly the dangers involved with possessing money. However, God's Word does not say that having money or working to get it is wrong. Many people misquote the apostle Paul by saying, "Money is the root of all evil." But look again at 1 Timothy 6:10 on page 107, and you will discover an important distinction. Money itself is not the problem; it is our attitude toward it that causes trouble. There is nothing wrong with having money; the problems come when money has you.

Mere money never satisfies. If your reason for working so hard is to "keep up with the Joneses," you are on a destructive path. Furthermore, if you are working at an unfulfilling job, hoping that greater financial gain will compensate for your unhappiness in the workplace, you will inevitably be disappointed. Money and materialism never deliver what they promise.

Maybe that's why the young man in the following story was seeking something money can never buy: soul satisfaction.

THE MAN WHO HAD IT ALL— ALMOST

He was young, well-mannered, well-educated, and well-off. He was sincere, honest, and above reproach. Maybe he also had an engaging personality and a winsome smile. Certainly Jesus found him likable; He even tried to recruit him (Mark 10:21). He was the man who had everything—except eternal life. And he could have had that, too. All he had to do was get rid of his money and follow Jesus.

But it wasn't to be. Elsewhere Jesus had said that no one can serve both God and money (Matt. 6:24). Here was living proof of that principle. In coming to Jesus, the rich young ruler came to a fork in the road. He had to choose

continued

continued

which one he would serve—money or Jesus. Apparently he chose money.

Jesus never condemned people for being rich. Nor does Scripture condemn the possession or the accumulation of money. But Jesus warned people about what He called "the deceitfulness of riches" (Mark 4:19). He understood the powerful but ultimately fatal attraction of money as a substitute for God.

Jesus perceived that tendency in the rich young ruler. The man was placing far too much value on his wealth. So Jesus told him to give it away, to free himself from its entanglements. It's worth noting that Jesus did not give that same ad- vice to every other rich person He encountered. But it was a requirement for this young ruler.

There are many rich young rulers today, people who have or are well on their way to having relatively sizable assets. Some are Christians and some are not. But sooner or later they all must answer the question that this man asked Jesus: "What shall I do that I may inherit eternal life?" (Mark 10:17).

Jesus' response is still the same: there's nothing you can do, only God can give eternal life (v. 27). But He gives it freely and graciously to those who follow Him (vv. 29–30). However, that's especially hard for the rich (v. 23). They have a competing offer, and it's very attractive. ◆

 Mark 10:17–27

17Now as He was going out on the road, one came running, knelt before Him, and asked Him, "Good Teacher, what shall I do that I may inherit eternal life?"

18So Jesus said to him, "Why do you call Me good? No one is good but One, *that is*, God. 19You know the commandments: 'Do not commit adultery,' 'Do not murder,' 'Do not steal,' 'Do not bear false witness,' 'Do not defraud,' 'Honor your father and your mother.' "

20And he answered and said to Him, "Teacher, all these things I have kept from my youth."

21Then Jesus, looking at him, loved him, and said to him, "One thing you lack: Go your way, sell whatever you have and give to the poor, and you will have treasure in heaven; and come, take up the cross, and follow Me."

22But he was sad at this word, and went away sorrowful, for he had great possessions.

23Then Jesus looked around and said to His disciples, "How hard it is for those who have riches to enter the kingdom of God!" 24And the disciples were astonished at His words. But Jesus answered again and said to them, "Children, how hard it is for those who trust in riches to enter the kingdom of God! 25It is easier for a camel to go through the eye of a needle than for a rich man to enter the kingdom of God."

26And they were greatly astonished, saying among themselves, "Who then can be saved?"

27But Jesus looked at them and said, "With men *it is* impossible, but not with God; for with God all things are possible."

---

1. Jesus did not command those who wanted to follow Him to rid themselves of their material goods. He did, however, tell the rich young ruler to sell his possessions and give the profits to the poor before pursuing a relationship with Christ. Why do you think Jesus did this?

2. Name some things that God has given to you which can be used to glorify Him.

_____

_____

3. What do you think Jesus meant when He said it was hard for a rich person to enter the kingdom of God?

_____

_____

◆ Commercialism versus Contentment ◆

Contentment doesn't come easily, especially if you are exposed to advertising hype by reading a newspaper or magazine, listening to the radio, or watching television. The advertising industry feeds our insatiable desire for more "stuff."

The next time you sit down to watch a program on television, notice how the commercials attempt to exploit our propensity for self-indulgence. Hour after hour, advertisements tempt and tantalize you with tasty morsels, served with the subtle promise that if you simply purchase this product, the "good life" will follow.

The apostle Paul never faced the advertising monster, but he did have to deal with the desires for the good life. Paul had wealth, power, and prestige; he also knew the horrors of abuse. Through it all Paul discovered the secret to a contented lifestyle.

A LIFESTYLE OF CONTENTMENT

Paul sounds so positive in Philippians 4:10–13, so confident! It would be easy to assume that life was rosy when he wrote these words. But where was he? According to 1:12–14, in prison—quite possibly in Rome, facing a death sentence!

Given that sobering context, this passage speaks powerfully to the issue of contentment, not only with material possessions, but with circumstances as well. Paul makes no idle boast here. He knew firsthand the wealth and privileges of prominence in the Jewish community and of Roman citizenship (3:4–6; Acts 22:3–5, 25–29; 26:4–5). On the other hand, he had suffered extraordinary hardships in his work—jailings, beatings, stonings, forcible ejection from several towns, shipwrecks—to say nothing of emotional and spiritual disappointments and setbacks (2 Cor. 11:23–33).

Either extreme would test a person's character. What was Paul's secret? "Christ who strengthens me." Rather

continued

continued
than looking to the possessions he had or didn't have, or to his circumstances, good or bad, he looked to Christ to satisfy his needs. The result, he says, was contentment.

This passage poses a strong challenge to Christians living and working in today's society. Some of us live at the upper levels of material *prosperity—"abounding," as Paul puts it. The temptation is to forget God (Luke 12:16–21). Likewise, much in our culture urges us to feel discontent with our lot—to long for more, for bigger, for better. Jesus warns against that attitude. On the other hand, failures and disappointments can also draw us away from trusting in the God who cares .* ◆

 Philippians 4:10–13

¹⁰But I rejoiced in the Lord greatly that now at last your care for me has flourished again; though you surely did care, but you lacked opportunity. ¹¹Not that I speak in regard to need, for I have learned in whatever state I am, to be content: ¹²I know how to be abased, and I know how to abound. Everywhere and in all things I have learned both to be full and to be hungry, both to abound and to suffer need. ¹³I can do all things through Christ who strengthens me.

1. What do you regard as your greatest strength in handling money? your greatest weakness?

2. In Philippians 4:13, Paul proclaimed that his secret to a lifestyle of contentment was "Christ who strengthens me." In what areas do you want Christ to strengthen you?

♦ ♦ ♦ ♦ ♦ ♦ ♦ ♦ ♦

Money pressures can place an enormous strain upon even the best relationships at work and at home. But God wants you to control your money, instead of letting your money control you. God wants you to live within your means and to have enough left over to help others when you can.

In the area of finances, as well as in every other area of life, it helps to have another person assist you. It is encouraging to have a fellow believer you can look to as a model of how to live a Christian life.

We all need practical help from mature believers as we grow more like Christ. Once we've matured, we can serve as a mentor to someone else. In our next chapter, we'll take a closer look at how you can develop mentoring relationships—relationships that will last forever!

PEOPLE POWER

J im, I think I am going to have to quit my job," Eric lamented over lunch.*

"You what? Why?" Jim made no attempt to conceal his surprise at his young friend's comment.

"I just can't seem to close a sale," Eric explained. "I've been a sales representative for this company for nearly three months now, and I haven't done enough business to pay for my gasoline and hotel expenses."

"Give it time, Eric," Jim said encouragingly. "You'll catch on. I recommended you for this job because I believe you can do it."

"Thanks, Jim. I appreciate that, but I'm simply not selling products. I wish I knew what was wrong so I could try to correct it."

"Hmm," Jim said softly, rubbing his chin as he thought about Eric's dilemma. "I have an idea that might help. Why don't you come on the road with me for a few weeks? I'll work out the details with our boss so you can come with me to watch, listen, and learn. When we think you're ready, we'll let you make the sales to my customers."

"Jim, you're one of the top salesmen in this company. Are you sure you'd be willing to do that? Wouldn't you be giving your trade secrets away?"

"Not really. After all, we are on the same team. I'd be willing to teach you. Hey, it might even be fun."

For the next several weeks, Eric traveled with Jim on all his sales calls. Jim explained his secrets for closing the sale and he coached Eric on better ways of presenting their products. Most of all, he modeled what it meant to be a great salesman—he exhibited a love for his products and, more importantly, a concern for his customers' needs. Eric caught on quickly and as his confidence began to grow, he experienced greater degrees of success.

Once Eric returned to his own accounts, the two friends began to meet for lunch regularly, so Jim could continue to teach Eric more about their business. When Jim received his commission check for the sales during the time Eric traveled with him, Jim split the money right down the middle with the younger sales representative.

"I can't believe you are doing this," Eric exclaimed as Jim handed him the money. "You've already given me so much!"

"Well, you deserve it," Jim said with a smile.

◆ ◆ ◆ ◆ ◆ ◆ ◆ ◆ ◆

Jim and Eric's experience is an example of the age-old practice of mentoring. A mentor is a trusted counselor or guide who is willing to take a less skilled or less experienced person and show that person "the ropes." The mentor—typically older, wiser, and more experienced—imparts valuable information to the younger person, not by lecturing, but by setting an example for the younger person to emulate.

The Bible is full of mentoring relationships. But "kingdom-style" mentoring has a higher purpose than simply teaching job skills. Kingdom-style mentors teach us about life. Take a look at the examples of kingdom-style mentoring in the following article, and as you read look for some ways you can develop some kingdom-style mentoring relationships.

Mentoring, Kingdom-Style

Paul describes the powerful process of mentoring in 2 Timothy 2:2. Just as he had helped Timothy during a formative stage in his development, he challenged Timothy to mentor others, who in turn could become mentors and keep the reproductive cycle going. Christians today need to recover this pattern of older believers working with younger ones, which dates to the earliest days of the faith. Here are a few examples:

Jethro with Moses

A cattleman and father-in-law to Moses, Jethro took his overworked son-in-law through a performance review and taught him to delegate authority to associates (Ex. 18:1–27).

Boaz with Naomi and Ruth

A wealthy landowner and relative of Naomi, Boaz risked rejection from Jewish peers when he rescued the impoverished widow Naomi and her widowed immigrant daughter-in-law, Ruth. Ruth faced rejection among the Israelites but had respect and honor from Boaz (Ruth 1—4).

Deborah with Barak

A national leader and judge over Israel, Deborah guided Barak into battle and then accepted his call for her help, leading the campaign to victory over a Canaanite king. Together they celebrated in song, and the land enjoyed peace for 40 years (Judg. 4:4—5:31).

Barnabas with Saul/Paul

A wealthy landowner from Cyprus, Barnabas stood up for Saul, the persecutor-turned-convert, introducing him to church leaders and vouching for his conversion. Coached by Barnabas (Acts 4:36–37; 9:26–30; 11:22–30), Paul became an outstanding leader in the burgeoning movement.

Barnabas with John Mark

In a dramatic split with Paul, Barnabas took young John Mark home with him to Cyprus and rebuilt his confidence (Acts 15:36–39). Years later, Paul changed his opinion, describing John Mark as "useful to me for ministry" (2 Tim. 4:11).

Priscilla and Aquila with Apollos

Manufacturers of mobile living units (tents), Priscilla and Aquila drew alongside gifted but confused Apollos, tutoring him in the faith and then sponsoring his ministry (Acts 18:1–3, 24–28).

Paul with Timothy

Pioneering leader Paul recruited young Timothy and built on the foundation laid by the young man's mother and grandmother (2 Tim. 1:5). Enlisting him as a fellow-traveler and tutoring him in the faith, Paul guided him in his first major assignment, the multiethnic start-up at Ephesus (Acts 16:1–3; Phil. 2:19–23; 2 Tim. 1–4).

Paul with Philemon

Paul helped Philemon, a wealthy leader in Colosse, deal with a runaway slave who had broken the law. He recommended full acceptance—even as a brother in the family—rather than insisting on the usual retribution. ◆

2 Timothy 2:1–7

[1]You therefore, my son, be strong in the grace that is in Christ Jesus. [2]And the things that you have heard from me among many witnesses, commit these to faithful men who will be able to teach others also. [3]You therefore must endure hardship as a good soldier of Jesus Christ. [4]No one engaged in warfare entangles himself with the affairs of *this* life, that he may please him who enlisted him as a soldier. [5]And also if anyone competes in athletics, he is not crowned unless he competes according to the rules. [6]The hardworking farmer must be first to partake of the crops. [7]Consider what I say, and may the Lord give you understanding in all things.

1. One of the best examples of mentoring in the Bible (other than Jesus with His disciples), is the relationship between Barnabas and Paul. Barnabas had taken Paul "under his wing," introduced him to the early church leaders, and helped launch his missions journeys. The day came, however, when people no longer referred to the team as "Barnabas and Saul" (Acts 13:7), but switched the emphasis to "Paul and Barnabas" (Acts 15:2). How do you think Barnabas felt about that switch?

_____

_____

_____

2. Scan the information concerning these two men in the article, "Mentoring Kingdom-Style," on page 116. How did Barnabas exhibit the following qualities of a good mentor toward Paul?

CARING: _____

_____

CONVEYING KNOWLEDGE: _____

_____

CONFRONTING and CORRECTING: _____

_____

_____

CONNECTING: _____

_____

_____

_____

3. What qualities do you think Barnabas may have noticed in Paul that caused him to take Paul under his wing?

_____

_____

_____

_____

4. In your opinion, what is the most important difference between instructing and mentoring?

_____

_____

_____

_____

5a. Name someone in your workplace for whom you could be a mentor.

_____

_____

5b. How can you go about establishing such a relationship? (For instance: I could invite the person to lunch, or to a ball game, or some other informal activity.)

_____

_____

_____

_____

◆ Are You Unteachable? ◆

A man confided to a coworker that he felt he was in a rut. He said he didn't feel challenged anymore. They talked for a while, and the friend suggested, "Why don't you take a class that could teach you a new skill? Or, maybe you could find someone at work who would help you out."

The man gave his friend a look of despair and said, "I'd be a much better teacher than I would a student!"

Whether he realized it or not, the man was indirectly claiming to be better than Jesus. For even Jesus submitted to wise teaching. Maybe you've never thought about it, but there was a time when Jesus Christ was a student. ◆

JESUS THE STUDENT

What kind of student was Jesus? Did He come into the world already knowing everything He needed to know? Was He able to acquire knowledge without even studying? The snapshot of Jesus in the temple (Luke 2:46–47) suggests otherwise. Though He apparently held His seniors spellbound with questions and responses, He nevertheless went through a lifelong process of education, learning and growing through "on-the-job training" from expert teachers.

Luke paints a picture of Jesus as a model student. The rabbis He encountered at Jerusalem were the preeminent experts in Judaism who researched, developed, and applied the body of Old Testament Law and rabbinical tradition to issues of the day. Some were members of the council, the governing tribunal of Judea. These teachers were fond of waxing eloquent on religious and legal questions in the temple courtyard for the benefit of any who would listen (Matt. 6:5; 7:28–29; 23:1–7).

Nevertheless, Jesus made strategic use of these authorities during His visit to the big city for Passover. Now age 12, He was considered a man. So He went to the temple to learn all He could about the Law of God. He proved to be an avid student, listening carefully and asking questions about His "Father's business" (Luke 2:49). Rather than embarrass His parents and offend His teachers by spouting off what He knew, He humbly subjected Himself to the discipline of education (v. 51). His turn to teach would come later. For now, He accepted the role of a learner.

It's a good example for all of us who must go through school and learn on the job. Like Jesus, we need to learn all we can from the best teachers we can find, showing ourselves to be teachable, with an attitude of humility. ◆

Luke 2:46–47

⁴⁶Now so it was *that* after three days they found Him in the temple, sitting in the midst of the teachers, both listening to them and asking them questions. ⁴⁷And all who heard Him were astonished at His understanding and answers.

The Curve Breaker

Do you remember the Curve Breaker in school? The Curve Breaker was the kid who always scored the highest on tests. He turned in term papers three weeks before they were due and received straight As. The Curve Breaker may not have had many friends and he was always quiet in the library (Hey! At least you were *in* the library, right?). He was never late for the class following gym. Teachers always knew they could count on the Curve Breaker to come through when nobody else in class knew the answer to the question. You may have called the Curve Breaker "Teacher's Pet." ◆

◆ ◆ ◆ ◆ ◆ ◆ ◆ ◆ ◆

1. Thinking back, how did you really feel about the Curve Breaker?

_____ I despised that kid.
_____ I envied the Curve Breaker's ability.
_____ I admired the Curve Breaker.
_____ I felt sorry for the Curve Breaker.
_____ The Curve Breaker was my friend.
_____ The Curve Breaker was me!

2. Now, consider this: Jesus was a Curve Breaker, but He wasn't a "know-it-all" type (even though He *did* know it all). He had a sincere desire to study and learn from the best teachers available to Him. What are some ways you can follow His example in your workplace when it is time to learn a new skill?

_____

_____

_____

3. Why do you think Jesus submitted Himself to the teaching of mere mortals when, as the Son of God, He already had all knowledge?

_____

_____

_____

4. According to Luke 2:47, all who heard Jesus conversing with the teachers were astonished at His understanding and His answers. Why do you think they were so surprised?

_____

_____

_____

_____

_____

——◆ Mentors Are Servant-Leaders ◆——

Phil Cramer's company was in trouble. Costs of doing business had exceeded the annual projections. Coupled with an unforeseen economic slump and local employee lay-offs from other companies, consumer interest for Phil's products was at an all-time low. So was the morale of Phil's employees.

Although business was bad, Phil was committed to not laying off his employees, unless there was absolutely no other alternative. Times were tough enough for his workers; Phil didn't want to make things worse. He cut his own salary to equal that of his lowest-paid employee. He took off his suit coat and tie, rolled up his sleeves, left his cozy office, and went out on the front lines to work alongside his employees.

Joe Fenton had worked at Phil Cramer's company for fifteen years. Recently, he had become so discouraged that he began looking for another job. Like most of his coworkers, Joe had been coming to work and just going through the motions. They were waiting for the inevitable ax to fall.

But when Joe and his buddies saw the boss working on the line with them, something strange happened. "I looked over at Phil," Joe said later, "and there he was with sweat pouring down his face and I knew he was serious about saving the company! Phil's example inspired me to work harder and to stop wasting time. Later, when I found out about the boss's salary cut, I was embarrassed to think that I had been so negligent at work."

Phil's spirit, energy, drive, and commitment were contagious for other workers, too. Within six months the company's red ink turned to black . . . and not a single person had been laid off in the process.

Joe Fenton summed up what had happened: "Phil Cramer didn't blame us for breaking his business or try to motivate us with threats of lay-offs. He didn't lecture us about sacrifice and commitment. He showed it to us."

◆ ◆ ◆ ◆ ◆ ◆ ◆ ◆ ◆

True mentors lead by example. They understand one of the most elementary lessons of leadership, which is one that is widely overlooked. True leadership is not a position of privilege, but one of service. ◆

ELEMENTARY LEADERSHIP LESSONS

Leadership is often understood in terms of power, manipulation, assertiveness, and ambition. The literature of the work world is cluttered with "how to" books that profile the famous and successful who have fought and won by these cruel values. In the first century, the Roman Empire was dominated by very powerful and manipulative family dynasties riddled with competition, violence, greed, and dirty tricks.

But Jesus modeled a different way of leadership. Throughout the New Testament we are shown glimpses of His life and character. In them we discover a stark contrast to our world's soap opera of abuse and distortion.

Hebrews 5 is one such picture. It describes a true leader as a priest who is . . .

- focused on people and how they connect with God (v. 1).
- compassionate with the weak and ignorant (v. 2).
- required to face sin head-on (v. 3).
- not self-appointed, but rather called by God into his role (v. 4).

Jesus was the perfect priest (vv. 5–10). The writer admits that this portrait is hard to grasp (vv. 11–14). However, those who seek to grow into Christlike maturity need to consider it carefully. Jesus provides for those who seek His help. All we need to do is ask (Heb. 4:14–16).

Who are your heroes when it comes to leadership? Why? Do you aspire to a leadership style that lacks the character of Christ? Why not ask peers or friends what patterns they see in you? Use the evaluations of others to rewrite your agenda for growth. ◆

Hebrews 5:1–14

¹For every high priest taken from among men is appointed for men in things *pertaining* to God, that he may offer both gifts and sacrifices for sins. ²He can have compassion on those who are ignorant and going astray, since he himself is also subject to weakness. ³Because of this he is required as for the people, so also for himself, to offer *sacrifices* for sins. ⁴And no man takes this honor to himself, but he who is called by God, just as Aaron *was.*

⁵So also Christ did not glorify Himself to become High Priest, *but it* was He who said to Him:

> "You are My Son,
> Today I have begotten You."

continued

continued

6   As *He* also *says* in another *place*:

"You *are a priest forever*
According to the order of Melchizedek";

7who, in the days of His flesh, when He had offered up prayers and supplications, with vehe-
ment cries and tears to Him who was able to save
Him from death, and was heard because of His
godly fear, 8though He was a Son, *yet* He learned
obedience by the things which He suffered. 9And
having been perfected, He became the author of
eternal salvation to all who obey Him, 10called by
God as High Priest "according to the order of
Melchizedek," 11of whom we have much to say,
and hard to explain, since you have become dull
of hearing.
    12For though by this time you ought to be
teachers, you need *someone* to teach you again the
first principles of the oracles of God; and you have
come to need milk and not solid food. 13For
everyone who partakes *only* of milk *is* unskilled
in the word of righteousness, for he is a babe.
14But solid food belongs to those who are of
full age, *that is*, those who by reason of use have
their senses exercised to discern both good and
evil.

1. List some great leaders whom you admire, along with the qualities they have displayed that you would like to emulate.

_____

_____

_____

_____

2. Hebrews 5:1–10 describes Jesus as the perfect priest who served His people. What qualities or principles can you find in Christ's example that provide a model for mentors?

_____

_____

_____

_____

3. What does it mean for a believer to become "dull of hearing" (5:11), and how do you think that could happen?

_____

_____

_____

_____

4. According to verses 12–14, some of these Jewish believers should have been teaching others by this point in their Christian experience. Why weren't they?

_____

_____

_____

_____

———◆ You Can't Do Everything! ◆———

Okay, let's face it. There is only so much work you can do in a day. Unfortunately, you can't always do everything that you need or want to. There will always be somebody else to see, another phone call to make, another report to do, or another letter to write. You can't possibly do it all. Maybe that's why Jesus didn't accomplish His work all by Himself (although He could have).

Instead, Jesus provided a model for us by delegating responsibilities—real responsibilities, not token tasks of tedium—to the men He was mentoring. Jesus assisted His disciples by encouraging their efforts. Risky business? Maybe. But Jesus felt that delegation of responsibilities and affirmation of His disciples' faith was the best way to reach the world. It still is.

DELEGATION AND AFFIRMATION

Is delegation hard for you? When faced with a choice between letting others do a task or doing it yourself, do you tend to sigh, "It's easier to do it myself"? Do you give others, such as coworkers, relatives, or friends, not only the responsibility but the needed authority to get the job done—even if it means seeing it done their way instead of yours?

Certainly Jesus had more reason than any of us to avoid delegating His work to others. When it came to proclaiming His kingdom, He had every right to lack confidence in His band of followers. He had experienced their failings firsthand (Luke 9:10–50). Yet He sent out seventy workers with full appointment to preach and heal on His behalf (10:1, 16).

In doing so, Jesus affirmed the often heard but less often practiced concept of people and their development as the most important task of a manager. Certainly He gave the seventy workers detailed instructions before sending

continued

continued

them off (vv. 2–12). But a study of His discipleship methods shows that He was just as concerned with their growth as He was that the task be accomplished or done in a certain way.

Jesus accomplished the work He came to do. He hardly needed seventy neophytes to help Him!

But He was clear that people matter, and that His disciples would grow only if they held real responsibility and authority. No wonder the seventy returned "with joy," excited by their experiences (v. 17). They would never be the same again.

Whom do you need to give more responsibility to and affirm with greater encouragement? ◆

 Luke 10:1–20

¹After these things the Lord appointed seventy others also, and sent them two by two before His face into every city and place where He Himself was about to go. ²Then He said to them, "The harvest truly *is* great, but the laborers *are* few; therefore pray the Lord of the harvest to send out laborers into His harvest. ³Go your way; behold, I send you out as lambs among wolves. ⁴Carry neither money bag, knapsack, nor sandals; and greet no one along the road. ⁵But whatever house you enter, first say, 'Peace to this house.' ⁶And if a son of peace is there, your peace will rest on it; if not, it will return to you. ⁷And remain in the same house, eating and drinking such things as they give, for the laborer is worthy of his wages. Do not go from house to house. ⁸Whatever city you enter, and they receive you, eat such things as are set before you. ⁹And heal the sick there, and say to them, 'The kingdom of God has come near to you.' ¹⁰But whatever city you enter, and they do not receive you, go out into its streets and say, ¹¹'The very dust of your city which clings to us we wipe off against you. Nevertheless know this, that the kingdom of God has come near you.' ¹²But I

say to you that it will be more tolerable in that Day for Sodom than for that city.

¹³"Woe to you, Chorazin! Woe to you, Bethsaida! For if the mighty works which were done in you had been done in Tyre and Sidon, they would have repented long ago, sitting in sackcloth and ashes. ¹⁴But it will be more tolerable for Tyre and Sidon at the judgment than for you. ¹⁵And you, Capernaum, who are exalted to heaven, will be brought down to Hades. ¹⁶He who hears you hears Me, he who rejects you rejects Me, and he who rejects Me rejects Him who sent Me."

¹⁷Then the seventy returned with joy, saying, "Lord, even the demons are subject to us in Your name."

¹⁸And He said to them, "I saw Satan fall like lightning from heaven. ¹⁹Behold, I give you the authority to trample on serpents and scorpions, and over all the power of the enemy, and nothing shall by any means hurt you. ²⁰Nevertheless do not rejoice in this, that the spirits are subject to you, but rather rejoice because your names are written in heaven."

◆ ◆ ◆ ◆ ◆ ◆ ◆ ◆ ◆

1. Many people are reluctant to delegate responsibilities and authority, especially in the workplace. Check the statements that reflect your opinion of delegation.

_____ I'm afraid that the job won't get done in the same way I would do it.
_____ I'm doubtful that the job will get done at all.
_____ It will take more time to teach someone else how to do the work than it will take me to do it myself.
_____ I don't have time to clean up a coworker's messes.
_____ I want the credit.

2. In Luke 10:1, why do you think Jesus delegated His work to seventy other workers rather than doing it Himself?

_____

_____

3. Although Jesus shared the workers' joy from their accomplishments, He gently corrected their misguided enthusiasm (vv. 17–20). List some possible reasons why He may have applied these corrective measures at this point?

_____

_____

_____

4. Where is the harvest that Jesus speaks of in verse 2? What is the harvest in your life?

_____

_____

_____

◆ ◆ ◆ ◆ ◆ ◆ ◆ ◆ ◆

The making of disciples and being a mentor to them was a priority for Jesus. Consequently, it must be a priority for us as well. Since the most effective mentoring relationships involve people with whom you have regular contact, it is only natural to seek out such a relationship with a coworker.

Mentoring shows the practical side of a relationship with Christ. The believer in the workplace has a perfect opportunity to display how faith relates to everyday responsibilities. Mentoring cannot be reduced to a simple program; it is a way of life. It is modeling Jesus for your coworkers, friends, and family.

Unquestionably one of the most difficult, yet most rewarding, areas in which we are called to represent Christ and make disciples is within our own families. In this day and age when the traditional nuclear family and "family values" are under attack, you will need all the help you can get in balancing work and family responsibilities. And that is precisely what our next chapter provides.

WORKING ON THE FAMILY FRONT

What man in his right mind would walk away from a $600,000-a-year career for the sake of his family? All-star major league baseball pitcher Tim Burke did. And, he gave it up while he was at the top of his game and getting better.

Why? Because his wife and their four adopted children needed him. Tim decided that being available to his family was more important than the glory, glamor, and big money of major league baseball.

How easy would it be for you to walk away from a high-paying job because of your family's needs?

_____ I could walk away with no hesitation; my family is more important than money.

_____ I would have to look for options that would allow me to keep the job, but I would have to make some compromises in order to care for my family.

_____ I couldn't leave the job. If I don't have the money, then I can't support my family.

♦ ♦ ♦ ♦ ♦ ♦ ♦ ♦ ♦

Maybe you have never had to choose between a job that pays over half a million dollars per year and your family, but the tension between the workplace and your family is almost palpable, regardless of your financial bracket.

The fact is, if you work outside your home (as most people do for at least part of their lives), you will probably spend as much time in the workplace as you do with your family. Conflicts between home and work responsibilities are inevitable. There will be times when a late afternoon meeting causes you to miss your child's recital. Or, there will be a business trip that makes you miss a family member's birthday.

No matter how hard you try to juggle all your responsibilities, someone will be disappointed because you cannot be in two places at the same time. Unfortunately, it is usually a family member who is disappointed.

We all experience such conflicts at some point in our lives. The importance of work responsibilities tends to overshadow our family obligations. Yet, the most important—and possibly most difficult and draining—work you can do is loving and nurturing your spouse and your family.

THE FAMILY: A CALL TO LONG-TERM WORK

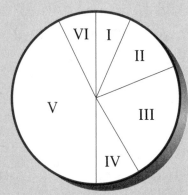

"Family planning" is a controversial topic today that evokes strong feelings and images. But there is a place for "biblical family planning" in light of the reality of family life as a decades-long process to which God calls His people. Indeed, the family, along with work, is a focal point of life as God has designed it. That's why Paul devoted so much space in Ephesians to the issues of married couples (5:22–33), children (6:1–3), and fathers (6:4).

If a couple marry in their mid-20s and live into their mid-70s still married, they will spend 50 or more years of life together. That's a substantial commitment! One would never enter a business contract for that length of time without clarifying the work and costs involved. Yet do young people have any idea of the lifetime of work they are taking on when they repeat their marriage vows? Often not.

Perhaps it would help to know that there are roughly six phases of marriage. Each one requires husband and wife to work together as a team, combining their unique temperaments and strengths. As with any team activity, they must pull in the same direction if they expect to complete all six phases with their marriage intact.

Of course, not every couple or family follows the pattern outlined below. But what matters is not that a family adhere to a certain timetable, but that it recognize that there are seasons of family life, and that building relationships is a lifelong process. The following six periods are by no means distinct categories, but overlap quite a bit.

I. The Honeymoon Years

During this first period of marriage, two people from different family experiences and value systems begin to discover one another. Dif-

ferences and similarities surface in areas such as finances, sexuality, faith, use of time, and personal habits. Each difference affords an opportunity for conflict and, hopefully, growth. Patterns that the couple establishes during this phase will tend to affect what happens during the next five phases.

The honeymoon typically ends with the birth or adoption of the first child. For some, it ends with the realization that there will be no children. In all too many cases, it ends with the dissolution of the marriage itself.

II. The Childbearing Years

The birth or adoption of the first child brings a rapid transition. New babies, though welcome, can feel like an "invasion," an abrupt intrusion into what up until then had been a relatively cozy twosome. Often the father particularly feels displaced as mother and infant bond through birth, nursing, and nurturing.

The childbearing years can be extraordinarily draining. Young parents often give out more than they take in from their children. They may be able to offset the deficit somewhat by revisiting some of the practices that they so valued during the "courtship" and "honeymoon" phases of their relationship. They'll need to "deposit"

continued

continued

lots of emotional support into each other's "reserve bank accounts" if they hope to maintain a positive balance during the demanding child-focused years. This period typically ends when the last child begins school.

III. The Child-rearing Years

As a couple's children pass through elementary and high school, new authority figures emerge, such as teachers, television personalities, scoutmasters, coaches, music teachers, youth pastors, and perhaps most influential of all, peers, both friends and bullies. Before, parents had the final word. Now others suggest or impose new values, decisions, and schedules.

That makes child rearing a great time for parents to help children think about themselves and the world. Discussion, prayer, and support can create an atmosphere of unity that is essential if young people are to face the many factors that compete with the family. If the parents are secure in their "bond of perfection," they can help their children tackle the tough issues—issues they themselves have been dealing with all along.

During the child-rearing years, which may stretch out over two decades or more, parents need to keep making deposits in their mate's bank of emotional support. One way to do that is to keep dating and to guard time alone with each other. Again, too many marriages never make it through the stresses and strains of the childbearing and child-rearing phases, and the families break apart.

IV. The Child-launching Years

With the onset of puberty, children begin to notice the opposite sex and discover "love" outside the home. This is the beginning of the "leaving" process, as children become adults in their own right and take steps toward independence, usually through work, college, and/or marriage.

In this phase, young adults tend to experience numerous "trial runs" of freedom, not all of which succeed. It helps for parents to remain available when their children have lost their way. Failure, whether in academic studies, financial matters, experiments in "freedom," or sexuality, offer important moments for learning, and sometimes for forgiveness. If young people never experience the freedom to fail, they may never learn to leave the nest and fly on their own.

V. The Empty-Nest Years

They're gone! Now it's just two again. Now the couple will find out whether they've grown together or apart over the years. Unfortunately, by this point many couples have developed a child- or career-centered marriage rather than a strong relationship between themselves. Though understandable, that can be tragic since the empty-nest phase typically outlasts the first four phases combined. No wonder so many marriages come apart as soon as the children have grown up and left. The couples have built their lives around their kids, and now they have nothing left in common.

By contrast, though, empty-nest couples who have built into each other can experience a joyous recovery of full attention to their marriage. They have more time to spend with each other, and often more money to spend. They may also have the bright privilege of welcoming grandchildren into the world.

VI. The Alone Years

The death of either spouse brings the survivor into the final phase of family life. For so many years, the person has lived in relation to his or her mate and children. Now, the sudden experience of being alone again exposes the level of individual growth experienced during marriage. Some couples never establish patterns that make for strong individuality. They become so intertwined and dependent on each other that the loss of the partner causes the surviving mate to crash or wither. But if the person has cultivated other relationships among friends and family and developed personal interests and hobbies, life can still be somewhat joyful, despite the painful loss of one's lifetime partner.

Where is your family among these six phases of family life? God calls couples to a lifetime of work. Are you practicing "biblical family planning" with a view toward the long haul? ◆

Ephesians 5:22—6:4

22Wives, submit to your own husbands, as to the Lord. 23For the husband is head of the wife, as also Christ is head of the church; and He is the Savior of the body. 24Therefore, just as the church is subject to Christ, so *let* the wives *be* to their own husbands in everything.

25Husbands, love your wives, just as Christ also loved the church and gave Himself for her, 26that He might sanctify and cleanse her with the washing of water by the word, 27that He might present her to Himself a glorious church, not having spot or wrinkle or any such thing, but that she should be holy and without blemish. 28So husbands ought to love their own wives as their own bodies; he who loves his wife loves himself. 29For no one ever hated his own flesh, but nourishes and cherishes it, just as the Lord *does* the church. 30For we are members of His body, of His flesh and of His bones. 31"For this reason a man shall leave his father and mother and be joined to his wife, and the two shall become one flesh." 32This is a great mystery, but I speak concerning Christ and the church. 33Nevertheless let each one of you in particular so love his own wife as himself, and let the wife *see* that she respects *her* husband.

CHAPTER 6

1Children, obey your parents in the Lord, for this is right. 2"Honor your father and mother," which is the first commandment with promise: 3"that it may be well with you and you may live long on the earth."

4And you, fathers, do not provoke your children to wrath, but bring them up in the training and admonition of the Lord.

1. What song title best describes the phase of family life through which you are currently passing?

_____ "Everything Is Beautiful"   _____ "Climb Every Mountain"
_____ "I'm So Lonesome I Could Cry"   _____ "I Will Always Love You"
_____ "My Way"   _____ "You've Lost That Lovin' Feeling"

2. In Ephesians 5:22—6:4, Paul gives us some sound advice which will ensure success in our families. List what you consider to be the most important family principles found in this passage.

_____

_____

_____

3. What are some ways a husband can express Christlike love to his wife? Be specific in your answers. (For instance: He can go shopping for antiques with his wife, even though he classifies any item over ten years of age as a piece of junk.)

_____

_____

_____

4. What are some ways a wife can show respect to her husband? Again, be specific in your answers. (For instance: She can watch a sporting event with him, even though she has no interest in the sport.)

_____

_____

_____

5. What are some simple things you can do to lessen the competition between your work-place and your family relationships? (For instance: I could only work overtime when it is absolutely necessary.)

_____

_____

_____

◆ Family Feud ◆

Frank grabbed Sam's shoulder and whirled him around in the middle of the department store aisle where they were working. While Sam was regaining his balance, Frank pushed himself right up in front of Sam's face and roared, "Don't you ever talk about my brother like that again!"

"What do you mean?" Sam asked bewilderedly. "You're the one who said he's a jerk. I was just agreeing with you."

"Yeah, well, it's okay for me to call him a jerk," Frank replied. "He's my brother!"

◆ ◆ ◆ ◆ ◆ ◆ ◆ ◆ ◆

Sound familiar? I can pick on my family members, but don't you say anything nasty about them.

If the truth were known, we would see that all of us have some nastiness hanging in our family trees. Sibling rivalries, marriage conflicts, infi-delities, abuse, addictions— you name it, and unfortu-nately you can find it in the lives of fellow Christians. But the real issue is whether or not you are going to allow the issues in your family's past to destroy God's plan for your life. Will you be able to over-come the hurt, bitterness, and resentment and discover a restored, healthy relation-ship with your family mem-bers? ◆

FOR OR AGAINST FAMILY?

Conflict seems inevitable within families. Family members can always find something to disagree about—personal values, current events, politics, possessions, sex, money, feelings. Why do some of the most bitter fights occur between people who married for love? How can people who are so familiar with each other sometimes find themselves so far apart?

One reason is that families are unions of sinners, and sinners will be themselves no matter how intense their love and commit-ment for each other (1 John 1:8, 10). This has been so from the beginning: the first eight

continued

continued
families in Scripture displayed many kinds of dysfunction, revealing their condition as sinful human beings. Perhaps God recorded their stories to let us know that even though He instituted the family unit, families are made up of sinners who will inevitably hurt each other.

Was Jesus "too good" to associate with His family of origin? His words in Mark 3:33–35 might seem to imply that. But He was merely distinguishing between human expectations about how families should relate and what the values of the kingdom had to say about family relations. He was not against His own parents and siblings; He just wanted to stress obedience to God.

"His own people" had already shown that they understood very little about Jesus or the values of His kingdom (Mark 3:20–21). They were limited by their own sinfulness, and needed God's help like everyone else.

 Mark 3:31–35

³¹Then His brothers and His mother came, and standing outside they sent to Him, calling Him. ³²And a multitude was sitting around Him; and they said to Him, "Look, Your mother and Your brothers are outside seeking You." ³³But He answered them, saying, "Who is My mother, or My brothers?" ³⁴And He looked around in a circle at those who sat about Him, and said, "Here are My mother and My brothers! ³⁵For whoever does the will of God is My brother and My sister and mother."

1. The lack of faith on the part of Jesus' family members was not the reason He asked the unusual question in Mark 3:33. Look at the question again. What do you think Jesus meant by it?

_____

_____

_____

2a. Briefly describe a time when your obedience to God threw you out of sync with a family member. (For example: My brother asked me to "cover for him," but I didn't because I would have had to lie to my parents.)

_____

_____

_____

2b. How did you feel about the friction or distance between you and that family member? How did you reconcile the situation?

_____

_____

_____

3. What difficulties did you and your family experience when you were growing up? How did you overcome those difficulties?

_____

_____

_____

◆ A Commitment to Family ◆

Mary followed Jesus throughout the years of His ministry. She was at the foot of the cross the day Jesus was crucified and their love for each other was obvious.

James and Jude, brothers of Jesus, didn't believe in Him until after the resurrection. Ironically, both James and Jude went on to write books that are included in the New Testament. We can assume that James and Jude were able to restore their relationship with Jesus.

Your relationships with your family members can be restored, too. You can begin the restoration process through love and forgiveness. Remember, though, that real restoration requires a commitment—a commitment to Christ and a commitment to your family.

THE CHALLENGE OF COMMITMENT

Commitment is in jeopardy these days. Some even call it the "C" word, as if to shame it as something we won't even acknowledge. After all, the demands and costs are too great. Today, convenience usually wins out over the sacrifice involved in being committed to someone or something.

The situation was no less confused in Jesus' day. As He began to unveil a new way of life for His followers, critics appeared and challenged Him on the difficulties of keeping the marriage commitment (Matt. 19:3, 7). Even His disciples quivered as they perceived the costs of maintaining one's marriage vows (v. 10). Later, they wanted to send

continued

continued

away some bothersome children in order to deal with more "important" things (v. 13). It seems that Jesus was surrounded by men who were a little unsure about domestic matters.

The discussion of divorce followed appropriately on the heels of Jesus' remarks about the merits of boundless forgiveness (Matt. 18:21–35). What better way to lead into the topic of commitment? Jesus didn't ignore the problems and failures of human relationships. Those very shortcomings are what make forgiveness—and commitment—crucial.

Those lessons were reinforced in Jesus' next encounter, with a rich man who wanted to ensure his possession of eternal life (Matt. 19:16–30). The man proposed rule-keeping as the standard by which he should be judged, but Jesus countered with an appeal for service (v. 21). True wealth involved a higher commitment—serving the Lord and others rather than the idol of material gain (vv. 23, 29).

Followers of Christ need to be known for their commitment—to marriage, to family, to community, to work, above all to Christ. Such loyalty often means messy obedience, but it is the way of Christ. How desperately that is needed in a day when people make vows of convenience rather than commitment. ◆

◆ ◆ ◆ ◆ ◆ ◆ ◆ ◆ ◆

 Matthew 19:1–15

¹Now it came to pass, when Jesus had finished these sayings, *that* He departed from Galilee and came to the region of Judea beyond the Jordan. ²And great multitudes followed Him, and He healed them there.

³The Pharisees also came to Him, testing Him, and saying to Him, "Is it lawful for a man to divorce his wife for *just* any reason?"

⁴And He answered and said to them, "Have you not read that He who made *them* at the beginning 'made them male and female,' ⁵and said, 'For this reason a man shall leave his father and mother and be joined to his wife, and the two shall become one flesh' ? ⁶So then, they are no longer two but one flesh. Therefore what God has joined together, let not man separate."

⁷They said to Him, "Why then did Moses command to give a certificate of divorce, and to put her away?"

⁸He said to them, "Moses, because of the hardness of your hearts, permitted you to divorce your wives, but from the beginning it was not so.

⁹And I say to you, whoever divorces his wife, except for sexual immorality, and marries another, commits adultery; and whoever marries her who is divorced commits adultery."

¹⁰His disciples said to Him, "If such is the case of the man with *his* wife, it is better not to marry."

¹¹But He said to them, "All cannot accept this saying, but only *those* to whom it has been given: ¹²For there are eunuchs who were born thus from *their* mother's womb, and there are eunuchs who were made eunuchs by men, and there are eunuchs who have made themselves eunuchs for the kingdom of heaven's sake. He who is able to accept *it,* let him accept *it.*"

¹³Then little children were brought to Him that He might put *His* hands on them and pray, but the disciples rebuked them. ¹⁴But Jesus said, "Let the little children come to Me, and do not forbid them; for of such is the kingdom of heaven." ¹⁵And He laid *His* hands on them and departed from there.

Commitment or Convenience?

1. On what basis do you make your commitments? Rank the following factors in order of how they influence your willingness to commit to somebody or something.

      _____ Personal opinions of others
      _____ My comfort and convenience
      _____ Whether or not I believe the commitment to be God's will
      _____ A sense of responsibility
      _____ Emotional factors (It just feels right)

2. Why do you think people tend to be more reluctant to make long-term commitments today than in previous generations?

_____

_____

_____

_____

3. From Matthew 19:1–15, it is easy to see that Jesus took the matters of marriage and family very seriously. In Jesus' eyes, marriage was a permanent commitment, not a relationship of convenience. That's why He emphasized that marriage should never be entered into lightly. What mistake did the disciples make in their understanding of the Old Testament laws concerning divorce?

_____

_____

_____

_____

◆ God Is Pro-Family ◆

Has it ever occurred to you that the Bible begins and ends with a wedding? In the beginning, God performed the first marriage ceremony between Adam and Eve (Gen. 2:18–25). Granted, there were no ushers, bridesmaids, or expensive accoutrements, but it was a wedding, nonetheless. All of creation looked on as witnesses.

Don't be fooled by those who claim that marriage and family are nothing more than institutions of society, and that they are easily expendable. The family is God's idea. After a person's relationship with Christ, marriage and family are meant to be the most intimate and fulfilling relationships we can have. So much so, that throughout the Bible marriage is used as a symbol of our relationship with God.

THERE IS HOPE FOR THE FAMILY

The fact that John's vision ends in a marriage between Christ (the Lamb) and His bride the church (Rev. 19:6–10) offers great hope to families. In this world, almost every family experiences some pain and suffering in its relationships. After all, families are made up of people who struggle under the burden of sin.

Of course, things were not intended to be that way. In the beginning, God instituted the family when He created Adam and Eve and joined them together as "one flesh" (Gen. 2:24). However, their sin and rebellion against God brought havoc into their relationship and into all subsequent families. In their own family they soon experienced violence as Cain murdered his brother Abel, causing an ongoing cycle of trouble (4:1–16).

Even in a fallen world, however, God desires His best for the family structure. Scripture holds out great hope for the restoration of marriage. For example:

- It encourages parents to raise children in an environment of truth and integrity (Deut. 6:2–9).
- It offers a touching illustration of aid to a family devastated by death and the prospect of poverty (Ruth 1–4).
- It shows a family destroyed by senseless evil but restored twofold by a faithful God (Job 1:13–21; 2:9; 42:10–17).
- It affirms the beauty of sexual love within marriage in terms of passion, fidelity, and integrity (Song of Solomon).
- It encourages the restoration of broken relationships, just as God will do with His people (Hos. 1:2—2:23).
- It offers guidelines for marriage in terms of mutual submission, loyalty, love, and discipline for children that does not alienate them—a way of relating that is similar to Christ's relationship to His bride the church (Eph. 5:22—6:4).

God's original design for the family will not be destroyed. Right now you may be experiencing the struggle of human relationships or even the pain of a broken family. But you can take hope from the knowledge that God's healing and love will ultimately win out, and He will "wipe away every tear . . . there shall be no more death, nor sorrow, nor crying" (Rev. 21:4). ◆

Revelation 19:6–10

⁶And I heard, as it were, the voice of a great multitude, as the sound of many waters and as the sound of mighty thunderings, saying, "Alleluia! For the Lord God Omnipotent reigns! ⁷Let us be glad and rejoice and give Him glory, for the marriage of the Lamb has come, and His wife has made herself ready." ⁸And to her it was granted to be arrayed in fine linen, clean and bright, for the fine linen is the righteous acts of the saints.

⁹Then he said to me, "Write: 'Blessed *are* those who are called to the marriage supper of the Lamb!' " And he said to me, "These are the true sayings of God." ¹⁰And I fell at his feet to worship him. But he said to me, "See *that you do* not *do that!* I am your fellow servant, and of your brethren who have the testimony of Jesus. Worship God! For the testimony of Jesus is the spirit of prophecy."

1. How does the fact that God is pro-family encourage you?

_____

_____

_____

2. What struggles are you currently experiencing in your family? How can your faith in God bring you through these situations?

_____

_____

_____

3. How does one receive and respond to an invitation to "the marriage supper of the Lamb" (19:9)?

_____

_____

_____

◆ ◆ ◆ ◆ ◆ ◆ ◆ ◆

The Christian life was never intended to be lived only in the realm of emotions. Being a believer is a matter of your will. You must decide to follow Jesus; you must commit yourself to living for Him. Only then is your reservation at the marriage supper of the Lamb secured.

On the human level, marriage and family are symbols of the believer's relationship to Christ. That's why it is important to keep your priorities straight in regard to your work and your family. Your family members must always know that in your heart and mind, they take precedence over your work.

Commitment to the family is one of the many convictions a believer must not compromise in the workplace. What you do flows out of what you are. As such, the convictions that you express in the workplace will have an eternal effect. In our next chapter, we will discover some convictions you can live with.

TAKING YOUR CONVICTIONS TO WORK

In recent years, millions of people have become disillusioned by the increasing number of scandals that fill the newspapers and news programs. People we used to automatically trust—police officers, clergy, teachers—are now subjected to constant scrutiny and distrust.

Instead of wondering whom we shouldn't trust, we have begun to wonder whom we can trust. Consequently, people have become skeptical and pessimistic.

One of the biggest areas in which skepticism is rapidly catching on is in the workplace. According to recent surveys, nearly half of American workers classify themselves as skeptical. Not only do they mistrust government, big business, and the products they purchase, but they are also deeply suspicious of their employers and coworkers. Should we simply accept this skepticism as a part of life, or is there something we can do about it?

HONESTY AND ETHICAL STANDARDS

"ARE THEIR STANDARDS HIGH?"

Occupation	%
Clergymen	64
Druggists, pharmacists	61
Medical doctors	53
Dentists	51
College teachers	47
Engineers	46
Policemen	42
Bankers	38
TV reporters, commentators	33
Funeral directors	29
Newspaper reporters	26
Lawyers	24
Stockbrokers	19
Business executives	18
Senators	17
Building contractors	17
Local political officeholders	16
Congressmen	14
Realtors	13
State political officeholders	13
Insurance salesmen	13
Labor union leaders	12
Advertising practitioners	8
Car salesmen	6

Paul called his generation "crooked and perverse" (Phil. 2:15). But was his generation much different than ours? According to the Gallup Poll:

By a large margin the U.S. public believes that ethics and standards of honesty are getting worse. This is a view held by all age groups and in each socio-economic level.

The public also does not give very high marks to people in most of the 24 occupations tested in a Gallup Poll in terms of honesty and ethical standards. On the left is the full list, with the percentages who say the honesty and ethical standards are very high or high.

Given such a low opinion of the integrity of so many occupations, believers today have an outstanding opportunity to "shine as lights in the world" (2:15).

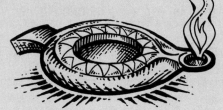

Philippians 2:14-16

¹⁴Do all things without complaining and disputing, ¹⁵that you may become blameless and harmless, children of God without fault in the midst of a crooked and perverse generation, among whom you shine as lights in the world, ¹⁶holding fast the word of life, so that I may rejoice in the day of Christ that I have not run in vain or labored in vain.

In the midst of this murky mess of shady morals, convenient ethical values, and skepticism, God is calling you to shine as a light. It is no accident that you work where you do. In fact, God has specifically placed you in a particular place to represent Him where you are. If your workplace does not have a very "spiritual" environment, don't despair. Keep in mind that even the smallest burning candle brings welcomed hope in the midst of great darkness.

◆ ◆ ◆ ◆ ◆ ◆ ◆ ◆ ◆

1. Why does Paul caution against complaining and disputing (v. 14)?

_____

_____

_____

2. Paul says our lives should be blameless, harmless, and without fault (v. 15). What do you think he means by that?

_____

_____

_____

3a. What is Paul referring to when he writes of running or laboring in vain (v. 16)?

_____

_____

_____

3b. How can you avoid laboring in vain when you work?

_____

_____

_____

4. In verse 15, Paul encourages us to be "without fault in the midst of a crooked and perverse generation." What does this mean? How can you apply this principle to your life?

_____

_____

_____

──◆ Is the Law Always Right? ◆──

We know that there are certain things Christians should and should not do. To some, it may appear that Christianity is simply a long list of dos and don'ts. It is a strict list of regulations that must be followed at all times. And, not only do nonbelievers sometimes see Christianity as a strict code, but there are also some Christians who believe this, too!

But being a Christian isn't that simple. There are many situations that are not handled by looking up the answer on a list of laws. These instances call for us to use our judgment and to deal with these situations in a way that reflects God's love and justice.

And doing this isn't always easy. In fact, many times we have to make tough choices. We must learn to balance our lives between following the letter of the law and following the spirit of the law.

THE LETTER AND THE SPIRIT

The Sabbath-day controversy (Luke 14:1–6) shows a tension between the letter of the Law and its spirit. The Old Testament was clear about keeping the Sabbath holy by resting from work (Ex. 20:8–11). But Jesus was known for doing the "work" of healing on the Sabbath (Luke 13:10–17). Was He breaking the Law or not? The lawyers and Pharisees couldn't say (v. 6).

Jesus let them stew over the issue, but clearly He was convinced that He was acting well within the Law. If He appeared to break it, it was only because His enemies paid more attention to superficial, external ways of "keeping" the Law than to its underlying moral spirit. Furthermore, over the centuries their predecessors had heaped up countless traditions on top of the Law, creating a mammoth set of expectations that no one could fulfill.

In our own day, even believers sometimes try to live by a rigid set of dos and don'ts that go beyond the clear teaching of Scripture. Like the Pharisees, we are tempted to be more concerned about the externals of the faith than the larger principles of "justice and the love of God" (Luke 11:42). Given His treatment of the self-righteous Pharisees, what would Jesus say to us?

Luke 14:1–6

¹Now it happened, as He went into the house of one of the rulers of the Pharisees to eat bread on the Sabbath, that they watched Him closely. ²And behold, there was a certain man before Him who had dropsy. ³And Jesus, answering, spoke to the

continued

> *continued*
> lawyers and Pharisees, saying, "Is it lawful to heal on the Sabbath?"
>
> ⁴But they kept silent. And He took *him* and healed him, and let him go. ⁵Then He answered them, saying, "Which of you, having a donkey or an ox that has fallen into a pit, will not immediately pull him out on the Sabbath day?"
>
> ⁶And they could not answer Him regarding these things.

1a. Why do you think the ruler of the Pharisees, a group openly hostile to Jesus, invited Jesus home for dinner?

_____

_____

_____

_____

1b. Why do you think Jesus accepted the invitation?

_____

_____

_____

2. What did Jesus' healing of the diseased man (vv. 2–4) have to do with the Pharisees' legalistic outlook?

_____

_____

_____

3. List some areas in which believers today go beyond the teachings of Scripture and establish their own sets of rules and regulations.

_____

_____

_____

_____

◆ Those Sticky Situations ◆

Carol was in a quandary. She was the only member of the small-town medical staff who was licensed to perform certain duties, yet her boss, Dr. Fuller, consistently permitted Carol's unlicensed coworkers to perform these duties.

She knew Dr. Fuller was trying to serve as many patients as possible and that he would never jeopardize a patient's health by allowing an inexperienced assistant to administer serious treatments. She was also aware that other doctors in the area allowed their unlicensed workers to do similar tasks.

Still, what Dr. Fuller was doing was against the law! And, by not reporting the unlawful practices, Carol was giving the impression that she condoned these procedures. She felt that she was compromising her integrity. But what should she do? ◆

◆ ◆ ◆ ◆ ◆ ◆ ◆ ◆ ◆

If Carol asked for your advice, what would you tell her?

_____ Obey your boss, even though he's breaking the law.
_____ Confront your boss privately about the matter.
_____ Threaten disclosure and possible legal action.
_____ Quit and find another job.

How are we supposed to judge another person's ethics? On the other hand, should we judge someone else at all? The Bible seems to present a mixed message by instructing us to "judge not, and you shall not be judged" (Luke 6:37) in one place, and to "judge all things" (1 Cor. 2:15) in another.

Which is it? Perhaps a closer look at the apostle Paul's words will help us better understand.

ARE WE TO JUDGE ALL THINGS?

Paul's claim about judging all things (1 Cor. 2:15) sounds rather presumptuous. Is he urging believers to become moral policemen, passing judgment on everyone and everything around us?

Yes and no. Paul was challenging the spiritually immature believers at Corinth to grow up by applying spiritual discernment to the world around them. In this passage he mentions three categories of people:

- *natural* (2:14), those without Christ, still living in the lost condition in which they were born;
- *spiritual* (2:15), believers in Christ who have been born of the Spirit and in whom the Spirit of God lives and is producing growth; and
- *carnal* (3:1), believers who remain immature in the faith because they don't allow the Spirit to work in their lives.

Spiritual people "judge" all things that come their way (v. 15) in the sense of scrutinizing, examining, and investigating spiritual value and implications. This is not something that we should do merely as individuals, but also corporately with other believers. For example, in the workplace Christians in various occupations need to band together to explore how the faith applies to particular vocations. By analyzing work situations in light of Scripture, we can discern what the issues are

continued

continued **and how we might respond with Christlikeness.** **"Judging all things" has nothing to do with damning others, but with recognizing**	**and doing what God would want. Instead of pride, it calls for humility, since God will be the final Judge of everything we do (2 Cor. 5:10).**

 1 Corinthians 2:13—3:3

¹³These things we also speak, not in words which man's wisdom teaches but which the Holy Spirit teaches, comparing spiritual things with spiritual. ¹⁴But the natural man does not receive the things of the Spirit of God, for they are foolishness to him; nor can he know *them,* because they are spiritually discerned. ¹⁵But he who is spiritual judges all things, yet he himself is *rightly* judged by no one. ¹⁶For "who has known the mind of the LORD that he may instruct Him?" But we have the mind of Christ.

CHAPTER 3

¹And I, brethren, could not speak to you as to spiritual *people* but as to carnal, as to babes in Christ. ²I fed you with milk and not with solid food; for until now you were not able *to receive it,* and even now you are still not able; ³for you are still carnal. For where *there are* envy, strife, and divisions among you, are you not carnal and behaving like *mere* men?

1. Describe the biblical difference between judging and condemning.

_____

_____

_____

2. What is the only accurate standard by which a believer can judge the validity of something or someone?

_____ Popular opinion
_____ The Bible
_____ Intuition
_____ Divine signs

3. What does it mean to have the mind of Christ (v. 16)? _____

_____

_____

_____

4a. What are some of the characteristics of the "carnal" person Paul describes in 3:1–3?

_____

_____

4b. What do you think causes these attitudes?

_____

_____

——◆ When We Just Disagree ◆——

Many believers get confused about the difference between biblical principles and their personal convictions. A biblical principle is something that the Bible specifically teaches that you should or should not do. For example, "You shall not murder" (Exodus 20:13) is a biblical principle. A biblical principle is standard for all believers, even though many may debate just how that principle is to be applied.

Personal convictions, however, are often matters of interpretation and personal tastes. They should not be considered standard for all believers. As such, you should not attempt to impose your personal convictions upon someone else, nor should you be pushed into accepting someone else's convictions as your own. When the Bible does not offer specific principles, we must all be tolerant of different choices and decisions made by fellow believers. Don't allow differences to divide us. Sometimes the only thing we can do is agree to disagree . . . but do it in love.

MATTERS OF CONSCIENCE

One noticeable difference between Christianity and most other religions is that Christians are not bound by ritualistic rules. Paul discusses two examples here in Romans 14: special days of religious observance (vv. 5–13) and food (vv. 2–4, 14–23). However, the principles he sets forth apply to all matters of conscience, the "gray" areas of life for which Scripture prescribes no specific behavior one way or another.

Special observances and food were apparently trouble spots for the Roman believers. No doubt those from Jewish backgrounds brought their heritage of strict Sabbath-keeping and were shocked to find Gentile believers to whom Sabbath days were inconsequential. Likewise, some from pagan backgrounds may have encouraged the church to form its own counterparts to the festival days they had practiced in their former religions. Either way, the keeping of "holy days" created tension in the church.

So did the issue of eating meat. The pagan religions of the day offered meat as sacrifices to

continued

continued

their idols. The meat was then sold to the general public. As it tended to be among the choicest cuts, it made for good eating. But many believers objected to eating such meat, or meat of any kind, lest they give tacit approval to the practice of idolatry. Others, however, saw no problem (v. 2). Again, Christians lined up on both sides of the issue. Predictably, people began to question each other's spirituality and dispute over whose position was "right" (v. 1).

Do these situations sound familiar? Perhaps meat sacrificed to idols is not an issue for believers today. But plenty of issues have managed to divide believers today. Does Paul offer any perspective on settling such disputes? Yes:

(1) No Christian should judge another regarding disputable things (vv. 3–4, 13). We may have opinions about what is right and wrong. But Christ is the Judge, for us and for others.

(2) Each person needs to come to his or her own convictions regarding matters of conscience (vv. 5, 22–23). God has given us a mind and the responsibility to think things through and decide what is best for ourselves in cases where the Scriptures are not clear. Unexamined morality is as irresponsible as no morality.

(3) We are not totally free to do as we please; we must answer to the Lord for our behavior (vv. 7–8, 12).

(4) We should avoid offending others by flaunting our liberty (v. 13). A "stumbling block" is an ancient metaphor for giving offense. It is easy to offend believers whose consciences are immature—that is, who lack the knowledge and confidence of their liberty in Christ (v. 2; 1 Cor. 8:9–12). This can happen in two ways: through trampling on their sensibilities by deliberately engaging in practices they find offensive; or through tempting them to engage in something they regard as sin. Even actions that are not inherently sinful can produce sin if they cause others to stumble.

(5) We should practice love, pursuing peace in the body and that which builds others up in the faith (vv. 15, 19). Christianity is just as concerned with community and healthy relationships as it is with morality. To be sure, there are matters that are worth fighting for. But where God is either silent or has left room for personal choice, believers need to practice tolerance and consider what is best for all. ◆

Romans 14:1–23

[1]Receive one who is weak in the faith, *but* not to disputes over doubtful things. [2]For one believes he may eat all things, but he who is weak eats *only* vegetables. [3]Let not him who eats despise him who does not eat, and let not him who does not eat judge him who eats; for God has received him. [4]Who are you to judge another's servant? To his own master he stands or falls. Indeed, he will be made to stand, for God is able to make him stand.

[5]One person esteems *one* day above another; another esteems every day *alike*. Let each be fully convinced in his own mind. [6]He who observes the day, observes *it* to the Lord; and he who does not observe the day, to the Lord he does not observe *it*. He who eats, eats to the Lord, for he gives God thanks; and he who does not eat, to the Lord he does not eat, and gives God thanks. [7]For none of us lives to himself, and no one dies to himself. [8]For if we live, we live to the Lord; and if we die, we die to the Lord. Therefore, whether we live or die, we are the Lord's. [9]For to this end Christ died and rose and lived again, that He might be Lord of both the dead and the living. [10]But why do you judge your brother? Or why do you show contempt for your brother? For we shall all stand before the judgment seat of Christ. [11]For it is written:

> "*As* I live, says the LORD,
> Every knee shall bow to Me,
> And every tongue shall confess to God."

[12]So then each of us shall give account of himself to God. [13]Therefore let us not judge one
continued

continued

another anymore, but rather resolve this, not to put a stumbling block or a cause to fall in *our* brother's way.

¹⁴I know and am convinced by the Lord Jesus that *there is* nothing unclean of itself; but to him who considers anything to be unclean, to him *it is* unclean. ¹⁵Yet if your brother is grieved because of *your* food, you are no longer walking in love. Do not destroy with your food the one for whom Christ died. ¹⁶Therefore do not let your good be spoken of as evil; ¹⁷for the kingdom of God is not eating and drinking, but righteousness and peace and joy in the Holy Spirit. ¹⁸For he who serves Christ in these things *is* acceptable to God and approved by men.

¹⁹Therefore let us pursue the things *which make* for peace and the things by which one may edify another. ²⁰Do not destroy the work of God for the sake of food. All things indeed *are* pure, but *it is* evil for the man who eats with offense. ²¹*It is* good neither to eat meat nor drink wine nor *do anything* by which your brother stumbles or is offended or is made weak. ²²Do you have faith? Have *it* to yourself before God. Happy *is* he who does not condemn himself in what he approves. ²³But he who doubts is condemned if he eats, because *he does* not *eat* from faith; for whatever *is* not from faith is sin.

1. The following are a few examples of personal convictions that can create conflicts for believers. Keep in mind that God does not give specific commands about any of these. Check any of these areas that you feel strongly about.

   _____ Tithing based upon gross income
   _____ Having a Christmas tree
   _____ Listening to rock music
   _____ Watching movies and television
   _____ Buying or selling on the Sabbath

2. In Romans 14:1–12, Paul lists at least four reasons why believers should accept one another, despite our differences. Write these four principles in your own words.

   (vv. 1–3) _____

   _____

   _____

   _____

   (v. 4) _____

   _____

   _____

   _____

(vv. 5–9) _____

_____

_____

(vv. 10–12) _____

_____

_____

3. According to verses 13–15, how can you avoid causing a fellow believer to stumble in his or her faith?

_____

_____

_____

_____

4. Paul encourages us to pursue those things that build up others (vv. 19–20). What are some practical ways you can build up fellow believers in your workplace? (For instance: I can compliment my coworkers on jobs well-done.)

_____

_____

_____

_____

——◆ It Really Works! ◆——

More than likely, we have all been angry at another person or hurt by someone else's actions. Think of a time when you were in such a position. How did you respond to the person who hurt you? Did you blow up, or did you hold your anger in and vow to get revenge? Did you confront the person and try to discover the reason for that person's behavior?

Each of us deals with hurtful situations differently, but there's one solution that applies to all disputes. That solution is to always forgive each other.

◆ ◆ ◆ ◆ ◆ ◆ ◆ ◆ ◆

PHILEMON

Does Christ really make a difference in relationships? Does He really bring healing and the resolution of old grievances? Does He really surmount differences in social and economic status? The letter to Philemon offers powerful evidence that He does!

THE BACKGROUND OF THE LETTER

Philemon provides a window on the story of Onesimus, a runaway slave, and Philemon, his master. The story begins with Paul's arrival in Ephesus. According to Acts 19:8–10, his work there for more than two years produced spectacular results: "all who dwelt in Asia [Minor] heard the word of the Lord Jesus, both Jews and Greeks."

Among those who responded to the gospel was Philemon, a wealthy man of Colosse, perhaps one of the many merchants doing business in the thriving economy of Ephesus. Philemon took his newfound faith back to Colosse and started or at least hosted a church in his home—perhaps the same group of believers to whom the letter to the Colossians was written (Col. 4:7–9).

Like most wealthy citizens of the Roman world, Philemon owned slaves. Scholars estimate that perhaps half the population of the empire may have been slaves. One of Philemon's slaves was Onesimus, possibly from Phrygia, the mountainous region in which Colosse sat. Whether Onesimus stole from his master, tired of his bondage, or thought he could take advantage of his master's new religion of love and grace, we don't know, but for some reason he ran away. ◆

THE PRODIGAL RETURNS

Years later, Onesimus surfaced in Rome— where he ran into Paul! The apostle was living in rented quarters (Acts 28:30), perhaps in the Greek-speaking section in south Rome, where Onesimus would likely have gone. Like his former master, the fugitive turned to Christ and began growing in the faith. Paul came to regard him as "my son . . . whom I have begotten while in my chains" (Philem. 10), indicating a close relationship of mutual affection.

But Paul faced a dilemma. Should he hold onto him? The fellow proved useful and loyal. That's what Paul wanted to do (Philem. 13). But by law he was required to return the runaway slave to his master, or at least turn him over to the authorities. Yet what would happen to this new believer, his spiritual son and friend? Would he be punished or sold? Could Paul live with himself, knowing that in a sense, he had betrayed the man?

Paul's solution was to send Onesimus back to Philemon—but not without protection. He assigned an associate named Tychicus to escort the fugitive back, and to carry three letters— two general ones to the believers in Colosse and Laodicea (Col. 4:16), and a personal one to Philemon. As the latter makes clear, Paul was leaning heavily on his history with Philemon. He was also counting on the master to demonstrate spiritual maturity by forgiving the slave and accepting him as a brother in Christ. No doubt Philemon's standing among the community of believers would add further leverage, as people would be closely watching his response. ◆

continued

continued

THE REST OF THE STORY

The letter to Philemon gives us only half of the conversation between Paul and Philemon. We don't know Philemon's response or what happened to Onesimus upon his return.

However, the name Onesimus appears among letters written by a bishop named Ignatius in about A.D. 110. Ignatius of Antioch was arrested and taken to Rome for trial. During the journey, he wrote a letter from Smyrna to the church at Ephesus in which he addressed the new bishop there, whose name was Onesimus. Many believe that this man was the same Onesimus who, as a slave, had run away from Philemon but later came to faith and returned.

Whatever the case, the Onesimus-Philemon story holds a number of significant lessons:

- It shows that in Christ, there is always room for reconciliation and a second chance for people.

- It illustrates how God works behind the scenes to bring people to faith and restore relationships.
- It shows the power of the gospel to work at a distance and effect change from city to city, coast to coast, and continent to continent.
- It shows the value of mentoring relationships, the way that older, seasoned believers can help younger followers of Christ work out problems and conflicts.
- It shows a measure of irony behind God's patience and providence: He had to send Onesimus thousands of miles away from his Christian master in order to bring him to faith!
- It shows that in Christ, people can change. Consider the many stages that Onesimus went through: from slave, to thief and runaway, to refugee, to convert, to penitent, to brother, and possibly to bishop. ◆

◆ ◆ ◆ ◆ ◆ ◆ ◆ ◆ ◆

LET ME PICK UP THE TAB

Paul tells Philemon that "if" Onesimus has stolen anything, he should send Paul a bill for it (vv. 18–19). But at this point he is writing somewhat tongue-in-cheek.

Paul knew that Onesimus really had "wronged" Philemon. Not only had he run away, apparently he had stolen property and owed Philemon restitution. Paul never questioned Philemon's right to have his slave returned or receive reimbursement for the theft. Conversion to Christ does not relieve anyone of obligations to others.

Nonetheless, Paul wanted Philemon to forgive Onesimus and receive him back as a brother (v. 16). But just in case the theft created a sticking point in the reconciliation,

Paul volunteered to pay for the loss if Philemon was unwilling simply to forgive it. (Notice how Paul was imitating Christ in this regard.)

Of course, Paul anticipated that Philemon would be more than happy to bear the loss. After all, he owed Paul a large, intangible debt of gratitude for all that Paul had done for him (v. 19). So in effect, he would be returning Paul a favor by accepting Onesimus back unconditionally.

Is there a lesson here about favors and paybacks? Consider: often when we impose on others, asking them to do favors for us or for our friends, our main concern is for our own interests. But Paul's main concern was for Philemon—not for his financial loss, which was trifling, but for his spiritual gain, which was considerable.

Philemon 8–21

⁸Therefore, though I might be very bold in Christ to command you what is fitting, ⁹*yet* for love's sake I rather appeal *to you*—being such a one as Paul, the aged, and now also a prisoner of Jesus Christ— ¹⁰I appeal to you for my son Onesimus, whom I have begotten *while* in my chains, ¹¹who once was unprofitable to you, but now is profitable to you and to me.

¹²I am sending him back. You therefore receive him, that is, my own heart, ¹³whom I wished to keep with me, that on your behalf he might minister to me in my chains for the gospel. ¹⁴But without your consent I wanted to do nothing, that your good deed might not be by compulsion, as it were, but voluntary.

¹⁵For perhaps he departed for a while for this purpose, that you might receive him forever, ¹⁶no longer as a slave but more than a slave—a beloved brother, especially to me but how much more to you, both in the flesh and in the Lord.

¹⁷If then you count me as a partner, receive him as *you would* me. ¹⁸But if he has wronged you or owes anything, put that on my account. ¹⁹I, Paul, am writing with my own hand. I will repay—not to mention to you that you owe me even your own self besides. ²⁰Yes, brother, let me have joy from you in the Lord; refresh my heart in the Lord.

²¹Having confidence in your obedience, I write to you, knowing that you will do even more than I say.

1a. Notice that Paul never condoned nor condemned the practice of slavery. Instead, the apostle cut to the heart of the matter by encouraging Philemon to forgive Onesimus and for Onesimus to return to his master. But in verses 15–16, Paul emphasized one major change that should take place in their attitudes toward one another. What was it?

_____

_____

1b. What should your attitude be toward those who have wronged you?

_____

_____

_____

2. What price was Paul willing to pay in order to see the reconciliation between Philemon and Onesimus?

_____

_____

_____

3. What are some possible sacrifices you may need to make in order to aid in the healing of relationships between your coworkers?

_____

_____

_____

◆ ◆ ◆ ◆ ◆ ◆ ◆ ◆ ◆

Let's face it. Being a Christian is not as simple as following a long list of rules. There will be many times when we are faced with situations that call for us to make decisions based on what we think will honor God.

The tough part is that there isn't always one answer to a question. God never commanded that His children look, act, or think in exactly the same way. Because of this, there can be more than one way to resolve difficult issues and still please God.

God does, however, expect us to be people of integrity who follow our convictions. He also expects us to accept those whose convictions are different from ours.

There will always be stresses, trials, and tribulations in your workplace. Competitiveness and jealousy may be directed toward you for no apparent reason. Nevertheless, as you continue to respond with grace, kindness, and love, God will give you the strength you need to overcome the trials, and He will even bring good out of what may have been intended for evil.

Will it be easy? No way! That's why you are going to need the encouragement you will find in our next chapter.

TACKLING TIMES OF TRIAL

Melanie saw Abby sitting alone at a table in the company's cafeteria. Melanie went over to join her friend for lunch. As she sat down, she said, "Hey, how's it going?"

"Just great," Abby cheerfully replied. "How has your day been?"

As the two coworkers chatted, Melanie noticed an odd look on Abby's face. There seemed to be a lot of pain lurking behind the normally lively eyes. "Are you okay?" Melanie inquired. "You don't sound like yourself."

"Oh, I'm just fine. I've been working too much lately. I'm just tired."

The two finished their lunches and returned to their desks, but Melanie couldn't stop wondering about Abby. Abby was *always* in a good mood. She was one of those people who never had a problem. In fact, things went so well for Abby that it didn't seem fair to everyone else!

◆ ◆ ◆ ◆ ◆ ◆ ◆ ◆ ◆

Have you ever met someone like Abby? People like this are always in a good mood; you never hear a complaint from them, much less see them get angry. Is it possible to live a completely trouble-free life?

While some people give the impression that they never have a problem, the truth is that they have their share of difficulties, too. They may like to believe that life is a bed of thornless roses, but no one can completely avoid problems. Problems are a fact of life.

And, if someone tells you that when you put your trust in Jesus your troubles will disappear, then that person is either naive or is lying. Scripture is full of illustrations of faithful individuals who experienced perplexing and distressing pressures in life. So will you, but Jesus will be there with you to help you through those stressful times.

WELCOME TO STRESSFUL LIVING

For many people in the world today, tension, conflict, weariness, and suffering have become commonplace. Nevertheless, some offer the vain hope that life's troubles can be done away with, that we can somehow get to the point where things will always be great. They suggest that faith in Christ will deliver us into a state of serenity and ease and bring prosperity, health, and constant pleasure.

However, that was neither the experience nor the teaching of early Christians such as Paul, James, or Peter, and certainly not of their Lord Jesus. Paul described the life of a servant of God in terms of tribulation, distress, tumult, and sleeplessness (2 Cor. 6:4–5). But he also linked these stress producers with rich treasures that money cannot buy: purity, kindness, sincere love, honor, good report, joy, and the possession of all things (vv. 6–10).

continued

continued

So as long as we live as God's people on this earth, we can expect a connection between trouble and hope. That connection is never pleasant, but our troubles can bring about lasting benefits:

Jesus *told us that if we want to follow Him, we must deny ourselves and take up a cross. If we try to save our lives, we will only lose them. But if we lose our lives for His sake, we will find them (Matt. 16:24–25).*

The writer *to the Hebrews encouraged us that our troubles are often a sign that we are legitimate children of God, who lovingly disciplines us to train us in righteousness (Heb. 12:8–11).*

James *encouraged us to rejoice in our various trials, because as they test our faith, they produce patience, which ultimately makes us mature in Christ (James 1:2–4).*

Peter *knew by personal experience the kind of pressure that can cause one's allegiance to Christ to waiver. He warned us that "fiery trials" are nothing strange, but that they actually allow us to experience something of Christ's sufferings so that we can ultimately experience something of His glory, too (1 Pet. 4:12–13).*

We *can count on feeling stress if we're going to obey Christ. But we can take hope! That stress is preparing us for riches we will enjoy for eternity.* ◆

 2 Corinthians 6:3–10

³We give no offense in anything, that our ministry may not be blamed. ⁴But in all *things* we commend ourselves as ministers of God: in much patience, in tribulations, in needs, in distresses, ⁵in stripes, in imprisonments, in tumults, in labors, in sleeplessness, in fastings; ⁶by purity, by knowledge, by longsuffering, by kindness, by the Holy Spirit, by sincere love, ⁷by the word of truth, by the power of God, by the armor of righteousness on the right hand and on the left, ⁸by honor and dishonor, by evil report and good report; as deceivers, and *yet* true; ⁹as unknown, and *yet* well known; as dying, and behold we live; as chastened, and *yet* not killed; ¹⁰as sorrowful, yet always rejoicing; as poor, yet making many rich; as having nothing, and *yet* possessing all things.

1a. According to verse 3, why was Paul careful not to offend anyone?

_____

_____

1b. How could he do this and still present Christ to a pagan culture?

_____

_____

1c. What does Paul's example suggest to you concerning your workstyle?

_____

_____

2a. In verse 4, Paul says he and his coworkers have commended themselves "in much patience." He then goes on to describe what "much patience" means to him and what he endured to develop patience. Which of these troubles were inflicted on Paul by others?

_____

_____

2b. Which of Paul's troubles were not caused by others?

_____

_____

3. Despite the many hardships Paul endured, how would you describe his attitude?

_____ Humble   _____ Malicious
_____ Depressed   _____ Revengeful
_____ Upbeat   _____ Joyful

4. How closely does your attitude compare with Paul's when you experience opposition, persecution, or tension?

_____

_____

◆ Tough Times Touch Everyone ◆

No matter how hard we try to avoid difficult situations, we all experience tough times of some sort. For many, a common response to difficulties is, "Why me? What did I do to deserve this?" But we usually can't find the answers to those questions. And, even if there is a cause for a problem, we are still faced with resolving that problem. All we can do is handle the situation with a positive attitude and move on. Besides, the Bible says that if we look carefully, we will see God's hand at work in our trials.

HUMAN RESOURCE DEVELOPMENT

God has a three-stage "human resource development" program for believers (James 1:2–5). Stage one involves *trials*—as many as we need, as hard as they need to be. That leads to stage two, *patience*—waiting for God with trust and perseverance. The final result is stage three, *wisdom*, which is God's goal of growth for personnel in His kingdom.

Do you want wisdom? Be careful when you ask for it! You could get a healthy dose of trials that demand patience. Eventually the process leads to wisdom—*if* you let it work.

James 1:2–5

²My brethren, count it all joy when you fall into various trials, ³knowing that the testing of your faith produces patience. ⁴But let patience have *its* perfect work, that you may be perfect and complete, lacking nothing. ⁵If any of you lacks wisdom, let him ask of God, who gives to all liberally and without reproach, and it will be given to him.

Notice that James does not say, "Here's some advice for you just in case you ever have a bad day . . ." On the contrary, James says, "Count on having various trials." It's not a matter of if you will have problems; it is only a matter of when. But the positive side of James' advice is that you can profit from the trials that cross your path.

◆ ◆ ◆ ◆ ◆ ◆ ◆ ◆ ◆ ◆

1a. What "trials" are you currently experiencing in your workplace?

_____

_____

_____

1b. What wisdom have you acquired (or do you believe you will acquire) as a result of these trials?

_____

_____

_____

2. Why is it possible for you to "count it all joy" (v. 1) when troubles come?

_____

_____

_____

3a. What is the difference between wisdom and knowledge?

_____

_____

_____

3b. What is God's promise to every believer concerning wisdom?

_____

_____

_____

_____

——◆ Jealousy on the Job ◆——

Ever since Martina had refused Rob's sexual advances at the company's Christmas party, Rob's attitude toward her had changed. No longer did he treat Martina with the respect you would expect between two equally-skilled coworkers. Instead, Rob belittled Martina's work in front of their boss, he spoke rudely about her to other coworkers, and he attempted to smear her name any way possible.

Martina maintained her composure at work and sought to counteract Rob's tactics by maintaining her impeccable performance at work. Still, she felt the stares and heard the whispers as she walked by her coworkers.

Finally, Rob went too far. He accused Martina of misappropriating company funds and taking the money for her personal use. Martina knew that she was innocent, and she could guess the reason for Rob's malicious attack upon her—but what could she do? The Christmas party incident had been strictly between her and Rob. She hadn't mentioned it to anyone else, so she had no proof of Rob's misconduct. She couldn't believe that Rob would stoop so low!

Unfortunately, there seems to be no limit to how low some people will go in order to get ahead or to undermine another's reputation and success. How can you deal with such maliciousness? ◆

Luke 20:20–26

20So they watched *Him,* and sent spies who pretended to be righteous, that they might seize on His words, in order to deliver Him to the power and the authority of the governor. 21Then they asked Him, saying, "Teacher, we know that You say and teach rightly, and You do not show personal favoritism, but teach the way of God in truth: 22Is it lawful for us to pay taxes to Caesar or not?" 23But He perceived their craftiness, and said to them, "Why do you test Me? 24Show Me a denarius. Whose image and inscription does it have?"

They answered and said, "Caesar's."

25And He said to them, "Render therefore to Caesar the things that are Caesar's, and to God the things that are God's."

26But they could not catch Him in His words in the presence of the people. And they marveled at His answer and kept silent.

RETALIATION FOILED

When highly competitive people are over-shadowed or intimidated they often resort to ugly tactics to try to regain their superiority. An unhealthy need for importance, success, and power can bring out the worst in anyone. Have you noticed this pattern among coworkers, family members, or yourself?

As community leaders saw Jesus once again gaining popularity and influence, they schemed to ensnare Him (Luke 20:9–19). They even enlisted agents for their plot (v. 20). Unfortunately, there always seems to be a ready supply of help for evil designs.

But Jesus refused to stoop to their methods (vv. 23–25). As they tried to undo Him, He foiled their plans with grace and truth.

Do you know how to respond to trickery or evil when it is intended for you?

In Luke 20:20–26, Jesus' enemies attempted to trap Him. Notice how they began the encounter by flattering Jesus (v. 21). While everyone needs a bit of praise and appreciation, we need to be careful about letting compliments "go to our heads." Jesus' enemies hoped that He would be side-tracked by their compliments, but that didn't happen. We need to be cautious of such tactics, too.

◆ ◆ ◆ ◆ ◆ ◆ ◆ ◆ ◆

1. Why do you think the spies' inquiry to Jesus regarding taxes was such a loaded question?

_____

_____

2. How did Jesus foil the efforts of His enemies and still teach an important principle about priorities?

_____

_____

_____

3. If you have ever been intimidated or "attacked" by a coworker, how did you respond?

_____

_____

_____

4. What actions could you take to help foil any injustices in your workplace?

_____

_____

_____

—◆ An Incredible Confidence ◆—

Pete couldn't believe it. He had been working at Acme for fifteen years, and his integrity had never been questioned. All of a sudden, his supervisor was holding him responsible for a missing shipment. His supervisor claimed that Pete signed for the shipment and now it was gone!

Pete tried to explain that he had never even seen the shipment; how could he possibly sign for something he'd never seen? But that didn't matter, and now his career was on the line. Pete didn't know what to do, except to continue to tell the truth.

◆ ◆ ◆ ◆ ◆ ◆ ◆ ◆ ◆

Have you ever been unjustly accused, betrayed by a close friend, or made to suffer because of the actions of someone else? Jesus experienced all of that, yet He refused to allow Himself or His disciples to retaliate with anger or violence. ◆

THE BLESSING OF A CLEAN CONSCIENCE

Would you feel free to welcome others to attempt to assassinate your character? Would you even help them? Jesus did. He had such a clean conscience and a secure trust in God that justice would ultimately prevail, and that His enemies could do no lasting harm, that He actually aided His accusers. He welcomed them (John 18:4), identified Himself for them (vv. 5, 8), and even protected them from retaliation by His own loyalists (v. 11). Jesus demonstrated grace in the face of hostility.

Jesus' innocence did not protect Him from suffering, pain, or death. But it gave Him a confidence rooted in a larger reality than life on earth. Because He answered to God's judgment (John 12:23–33; 14:1–4), He was free to suffer, even unjustly. He left justice up to God and did not resort to retaliation.

John 18:1–11

¹When Jesus had spoken these words, He went out with His disciples over the Brook Kidron, where there was a garden, which He and His disciples entered. ²And Judas, who betrayed Him, also knew the place; for Jesus often met there with His disciples. ³Then Judas, having received a detachment *of troops,* and officers from the chief priests and Pharisees, came there with lanterns, torches, and weapons. ⁴Jesus therefore, knowing all things that would come upon Him, went forward and said to them, "Whom are you seeking?"

⁵They answered Him, "Jesus of Nazareth."

Jesus said to them, "I am *He.*" And Judas, who betrayed Him, also stood with them. ⁶Now when He said to them, "I am *He,*" they drew back and fell to the ground.

⁷Then He asked them again, "Whom are you seeking?"

And they said, "Jesus of Nazareth."

⁸Jesus answered, "I have told you that I am *He.* Therefore, if you seek Me, let these go their way," ⁹that the saying might be fulfilled which He spoke, "Of those whom You gave Me I have lost none."

¹⁰Then Simon Peter, having a sword, drew it and struck the high priest's servant, and cut off his right ear. The servant's name was Malchus.

¹¹So Jesus said to Peter, "Put your sword into the sheath. Shall I not drink the cup which My Father has given Me?"

1. Is there an unjust situation occurring in your life or in your workplace over which you have no control? If so, briefly describe it.

_____

_____

_____

2. John 18:6 records what may be one of the most intriguing events in the entire Bible. Why do you think Jesus' accusers drew back and fell to the ground?

_____

_____

3. Why do you think Jesus rebuked Peter for attempting to defend Him (vv. 10–11)?

_____

_____

_____

◆ Trusting God for Good ◆

Many of us have been faced with the question, "If God is good, then why does He permit bad things to happen to good people?" Unfortunately, there is no easy answer. God is God, and He calls the shots. You could spend months debating God's permissive will, but when you get down to it, you cannot avoid the conclusion that God is in control and He is working through all things for our eternal good.

ALL THINGS FOR GOOD?

Romans 8:28 is easy to quote to someone else. But what about when it's *your* turn to suffer? Is there comfort in this passage? Notice two important things as you consider Paul's words here:

(1) All things work together *for* good but not all things *are* good. The loss of a job, a tyrannical boss, physical illness, or family troubles are not good *per se.* In fact, often they are the direct result of evil. That's important to observe. Believers are never promised immunity from the problems and pains of the world. Every day we must put up with much that is not good.

(2) Nevertheless, good can come out of bad! This verse promises that God uses all the circumstances of our lives—both the good and the bad—to shape outcomes that accomplish His purposes for us. And His purposes can only be good, because He is good by definition (James 1:17).

So how can you make this verse work for you as you face tough, troubling times?

• Affirm your trust in God's presence.
• Align your goals with God's purposes.
• Accept the reliability of God's promises.

Romans 8:28

> 28And we know that all things work together for good to those who love God, to those who are the called according to *His* purpose.

Notice that Romans does not say that all things will work out for our momentary happiness or our comfort or our convenience. Consider Scott, an accountant with a large company, who was fired from his high-paying job because he would not do some "creative adjusting" to the financial figures. Did Scott regard getting fired as "good"? No way! But he did believe that God would use the situation for good.

Not long after this incident, the chief executive officer of another company heard about Scott's termination. He contacted Scott and said, "We want people with that sort of integrity at our company." The CEO arranged to have Scott hired at nearly twice the salary he had been making.

Of course, not every story works out so nicely. But you can be confident that God will eventually make something good come out of that which may not appear to be beneficial at the moment. ◆

◆ ◆ ◆ ◆ ◆ ◆ ◆ ◆ ◆

1. Notice that the promise of Romans 8:28 is not for everybody. Who are those to whom the promise is guaranteed?

_____

_____

_____

2. Describe a situation, condition, or relationship in your workplace that currently looks as though not even God could bring good out of it.

_____

_____

_____

3. How can the faith that God will work all things together for your ultimate good give you confidence in the workplace?

_____

_____

_____

Jesus never said it would be easy to follow Him. Nor did He ever imply that you would be popular for wanting to represent Him in the workplace. But Christ did promise that no person would ever serve Him in vain.

Trials and tribulations may come—no, will come—but through them, God will teach us much about ourselves and much about Him. He will continue molding us and shaping us, getting us ready to spend eternity with Him.

TAKE THIS JOB AND . . . LOVE IT!

I t's hard to believe that twelve chapters about life in the workplace have gone by so quickly! Hopefully you have been refreshed by looking at work from God's perspective and by discovering new ways of demonstrating how to be a Christian worker.

This chapter is intended to help you sum up what you've learned and put it all together in your heart and mind so you can "take it to the streets." Hopefully, as you have progressed through this book, you have obtained some fresh ideas about how your relationship with Christ can grow deeper, how your attitude about work can improve, and how your convictions can become clearer.

Keep in mind, too, that the workplace is not limited to an office or a desk. Your workplace is wherever you spend most of your time, and it includes the people who surround you on a daily basis.

God will continue to guide you in your work as long as you allow Him to work through you.

◆ ◆ ◆ ◆ ◆ ◆ ◆ ◆ ◆

——◆ "But It's Just *Work*" ◆——

Perhaps you were surprised to discover in chapter 1 that God views your work positively. Because of a misinterpretation of the Old Testament regarding the fall of man, many believers have viewed work as a curse. The truth, however, is that God gave Adam work to do in the garden of Eden prior to the fall. The Bible says, "Then the LORD God took the man and put him in the garden of Eden to tend and keep it" (Gen. 2:15). Instead of being a curse, your work is a means of honoring God.

God intends for you to receive a great sense of satisfaction from your work. You don't need to quit your job and sign on with a foreign missions organization before your work will matter to God. By doing quality work, earning a reputation for diligence and thoroughness, and contributing to the team effort of your employer and coworkers, you are honoring God in your workplace. ◆

◆ ◆ ◆ ◆ ◆ ◆ ◆ ◆ ◆

1. How has the understanding that work is not a curse changed your attitude toward the time you spend at your workplace?

_____

_____

_____

_____

2. Since beginning this book, how have you been able to find a greater sense of joy in your work?

_____

_____

_____

3. How have you been able to honor God in your workplace?

_____

_____

_____

_____

——◆ A Commitment to Excellence ◆——

In chapter 2, we looked at the relationship between you and your boss, and we examined the question of who you are really working for. Whatever your job description is and whoever your boss is, Jesus is ultimately the One you want to please.

We also considered competitiveness among coworkers. Some competition is healthy; it urges us to strive to do better. But when we begin to resort to unethical means in order to get ahead, then competition becomes destructive. We forget (or don't realize) how our behavior hurts our coworkers.

One way to avoid this trap is to treat your coworkers as brothers and sisters rather than as competitors. Another way is by developing a workstyle that demonstrates Christlike behavior. Your honest, diligent, and scrupulous work habits will convey more about Jesus than anything you tell them about Him.

◆ ◆ ◆ ◆ ◆ ◆ ◆ ◆ ◆

1. How did the acknowledgment of having Jesus as your Ultimate Boss inspire you to be a better employer or employee?

_____

_____

_____

_____

2. Have any of your coworkers noticed a difference in your workstyle lately? How have they responded?

_____

_____

_____

——◆ More than Words ◆——

Before a believer's message about Jesus will be accepted, credibility must be earned through one's character, demeanor, and workstyle. This is true anywhere a Christian wants to be a witness for Christ, but, as we saw in chapter 3, it is particularly true in the workplace. Think about how much time you spend with your coworkers. If they don't see Jesus in you, how can they believe the things you say about Him?

To be effective as a witness in the workplace, you must take a personal interest in your coworkers. They are not robots who perform daily routines. Your coworkers are real people with real needs. If you are going to tell them about Jesus, you must start where they are and present the gospel message to them in a manner they will most easily understand and accept.

◆ ◆ ◆ ◆ ◆ ◆ ◆ ◆ ◆ ◆

1. How do you present Christ in the workplace?

_____

_____

_____

2. In what ways do you want to change your witness in the workplace?

_____

_____

_____

——◆ Don't Discount Diversity ◆——

Most of us tend to gravitate toward people who are somewhat similar to ourselves in conduct, values, and family background. In the workplace, however, you are mixed in with people from a wide variety of racial, ethnic, cultural, and religious heritages. As a result, the workplace can breed prejudice.

But it doesn't need to be that way. You can break through any barrier that is built by bitter biases. In chapter 4, Jesus provided an example of this when He did not allow longstanding racial and ethnic prejudices to prevent Him from spreading His message of love and forgiveness to the Samaritan woman (John 4:4–42).

The New Testament teaches that believers are one in Christ (Gal. 3:20), regardless of color, sex, nationality, or family background. We are all part of God's family. Where exploitation, prejudice, anger, resentment, and bitterness have raised their ugly heads in your workplace, God wants to use you as an agent to help stamp them out. But you won't rid your workplace of these moral cancers by shouting or threatening people. These prejudices can only be dissolved by demonstrating the type of acceptance Jesus showed us.

◆ ◆ ◆ ◆ ◆ ◆ ◆ ◆ ◆

1. What barriers exist in your workplace?

_____

_____

_____

2. What steps are you taking to break down these barriers?

_____

_____

_____

——◆ At Work in Your City ◆——

Have you ever attended a sporting event in a large stadium, looked around at the mass of people, and wondered, Does God really care about all these folks? Or, have you ever experienced the busy rush hour of a large city and wondered, Could God possibly be here? Sometimes the sheer magnitude of our population crammed into the limited space of our urban centers can overwhelm us.

However, in chapter 5 we learned that God cares just as much about people in cities as He does people in the country. In fact, Jesus did a lot of His preaching in cities. He knew that city-dwellers needed to hear the gospel just as much—if not more—than the folks in rural areas.

Yet for many contemporary Christians, the city is too big and too noisy. Brushing shoulders with people who do not share your cultural background may make you slightly uncomfortable. But as a believer in the workplace, God has given you an unprecedented opportunity to see literally millions of lives affected as the gospel permeates the fabric of your city.

1. What are you doing to help reach your city with the gospel?

_____

_____

_____

2. Name at least one of the needs in your city, and list what you could do to help alleviate that need.

_____

_____

_____

——◆ What Is True Success? ◆——

Money, power, prestige, fame—these are some of the responses people give when they're asked to describe success. But in chapter 6, we discovered that these are not God's definitions of success. True success has little to do with the financial bottom line; it does, however, have everything to do with obeying God's commands.

In our society, success carries a high price tag for many people. Some of our coworkers and friends work too much, play too little, and often allow their personal lives to slide down the tubes. Ironically, the obsession with success is not driven by money as much as it is a sense of inadequacy and insecurity. Deep inside, many feel they do not matter in life unless they achieve certain objectives. They feel they must do whatever it takes to prove they are successful, even if it means sacrificing their families, their health, and sometimes even their souls.

◆ ◆ ◆ ◆ ◆ ◆ ◆ ◆ ◆

1. What does being successful mean to you?

_____

_____

_____

2. What is your greatest ambition in life?

_____

_____

_____

_____

——◆ You're Not the Lone Ranger ◆——

In chapter 7, we examined the advantages of being accountable to God and to each other. In your workplace you are accountable to your superiors, to your partners or the stockholders, to your clients and customers, and to your coworkers. At home you are accountable to your spouse (or your parents if you are living with them) and your children.

Most of us don't particularly like to have somebody looking over our shoulders. After all, isn't independence one of the goals for which we are striving? Yet the Bible teaches that accountability (when it is functioning correctly) can help prevent us from making too many errors and can keep us from compromising our values. An accountability relationship doesn't need to be obtrusive. Sometimes it may be as informal as having someone love you enough to tell you the truth or to ask the tough questions.

We also noted that we are not simply accountable in the areas of work ethics, money, morals, and family relationships; we are also accountable to God for everything He has given us. The question is not how much you have, but what have you done with what God has given you?

◆ ◆ ◆ ◆ ◆ ◆ ◆ ◆ ◆

1. With whom can you establish an accountability relationship?

_____

_____

2. Have you initiated the process of establishing an accountability relationship? How do you feel about that relationship?

_____

_____

——◆ Money, Money, and More Money! ◆——

One area in which most of us could be a bit more accountable is that of money. Ask ten people from various financial brackets, "Are you having money problems?" The inevitable answer will be yes! How can that be? Simple—it is never the amount of money that causes the problems; it is what a person does with the money that makes the difference.

Money has a powerful presence in your life. Unquestionably, the temptations surrounding money and its use reach out even to those with good intentions.

In chapter 8, we saw that Jesus never exploited people's desire to be prosperous when He was recruiting disciples or preaching the gospel. In fact, He watched a rich young ruler walk away when the young man chose his money over following Christ. There's no doubt that the young man could have contributed a great deal to Jesus' ministry if Jesus had lowered the cost of discipleship; but He didn't. In the young ruler's attempt to save his money, he lost his soul.

On the other hand, the apostle Paul proved that it is possible to be content with or without money and possessions. Some people presume that if a Christian is financially well-off, then that person must be doing something wrong. But that is not necessarily so. Other Christians believe that material wealth is an indication of God's blessing, but that isn't true either. The Lord promises you an abundant life (John 10:10), but that abundance may not be measured by money. For many, the reward for faithfulness to God will not be seen until they arrive in heaven.

◆ ◆ ◆ ◆ ◆ ◆ ◆ ◆ ◆

1. Jesus said, "Where your treasure is, there your heart will be also" (Matt 6:21). What is your treasure and where is it?

_____

_____

_____

2. How important are money and material possessions to your contentment?

_____ Money is unimportant to me.
_____ I would still be content if I had less money than I do now.
_____ I would not be content with less money than I have now.
_____ Having money makes me content.

——◆ People Power ◆——

A good mentor is more than merely a good instructor. It is someone who teaches by example. A mentor models the teaching instead of simply talking about it.

A classic case of mentoring is Jesus and His apostles. He taught them the principles of Christianity by being with them and showing them the meaning of being a Christian. For three years the apostles walked, talked, and ate with Jesus. They watched many people bring their needs to Him and how He helped all who would allow Him to do so. They also saw Jesus when the pressure was on. Time after time when the Pharisees and other Jewish leaders attempted to trap Jesus, the disciples heard Him respond in wisdom and love.

After the resurrection, when the apostles went out to tell the world that Jesus was alive, they didn't simply recite answers they had memorized. They proclaimed the truth that Jesus had taught them with His life. No wonder their witness was so powerful.

The apostle Paul and his understudy, Timothy, also had this sort of relationship. Timothy learned about God from his mother; then he learned how to do the work of God from his mentor, Paul. Timothy went on to invest his life in a small group of leaders. As a result, those leaders taught another group, that taught another group, and the principles of Christian living were passed from person to person in ever-widening circles. Jesus' command to go and make disciples (Matt. 28:19) is still in effect today.

1. Is there someone in your workplace with whom you have already been able to establish a mentoring relationship? If so, what is that person's name?

_____

2. If you have not yet established such a relationship, list several people with whom you could establish a mentoring relationship.

_____

_____

_____

——◆ Working on the Family Front ◆——

The family is not an institution of society that should be considered useful as long as it serves our purposes. The family was instituted by God, and it carries His blessing like no other relationship on earth (except, perhaps, the church, which God also intends to be a "family affair").

We learned in chapter 10 that conflicts between family and work are inevitable. We spend so much time working, that it is easy to become wrapped up in the demands of work and put our family lives on hold. But families require a lot of attention, too. Unfortunately, we often find it easier to put our families' needs on the back burner, and in doing this we weaken precious family ties.

Think about this, though. One day you will not work as much as you do now. When that day arrives, will your family still be there, or will those ties have been broken by the demands of your work?

Believers don't get married and have children just for the fun of it. We marry and reproduce to glorify Jesus Christ. After our relationship with God, the nurturing of family relationships takes precedence over all other callings in life, including—and here is the tough part—the work world.

◆ ◆ ◆ ◆ ◆ ◆ ◆ ◆ ◆

1a. Do your family's needs take priority over your work responsibilities?

_____

1b. If not, what are you doing to adjust your priorities so you can be more attuned to the needs of your family?

_____

_____

_____

2. What are the benefits of putting your family before your career?

_____

_____

_____

——◆ Taking Your Convictions to Work ◆——

We discovered in chapter 11 that God binds all believers together, despite any differences that divide us. Yes, there are commandments that apply to all of us. But in many situations it's up to us to make decisions based on our convictions.

We really are brothers and sisters in Christ. As such, when our beliefs differ from a fellow believer's, we need to respect that person's decisions. Jesus never taught His disciples to focus on minor differentiations in their faith. He said, "By this all will know that you are My disciples, if you have love for one another" (John 13:35). What a powerful example you and your coworkers will set by laying aside personal differences.

We looked at a practical illustration of acceptance and forgiveness in the lives of Paul, Philemon, and Onesimus. Paul never condoned nor denied the wrongs that had been done; but he did encourage Philemon and Onesimus to forgive each other and to love each other as brothers in Christ.

◆ ◆ ◆ ◆ ◆ ◆ ◆ ◆ ◆

1. What steps are you taking to reduce any friction between you and fellow believers in your workplace?

_____

_____

_____

2a. How is your ethical integrity being challenged in your workplace?

_____

_____

2b. How are you attempting to meet that challenge in a positive way?

_____

_____

_____

——◆ Tackling Times of Trial ◆——

In chapter 12, we acknowledged that trials and tribulations are inevitable. The good news is that God will use all things to work for our good and for His glory. Through all the trials, Jesus has promised, "I am with you always, even to the end of the age" (Matt. 28:20).

It can be tough finding the good in some situations—especially in the competitive work world. Ruthlessness and selfishness sometimes seem to be ruling forces. Ultimately, though, those forces will be defeated. Your integrity is the best defense when you are faced with un-scrupulous situations.

◆ ◆ ◆ ◆ ◆ ◆ ◆ ◆ ◆

1. Think of the most recent time you experienced a difficult work situation. What good came out of that situation?

_____

_____

2. In the future, how will you act when faced with troubling circumstances?

_____

_____

——◆ A New Outlook on Work ◆——

Work is not a meaningless way to pass the time. Your work matters to God; He cares about what you do and how you do it. Work can be very fulfilling and it can give you a sense of accomplishment.

But remember, your work does not determine your value as a person. Your life has innate value to God. In His eyes, your value or success is not measured by material wealth.

As Christians, we are called to live our lives with such honesty and integrity that everyone can see God working in us. We may not be able to change certain unpleasant circumstances in the workplace, but we can change our attitudes and actions. It is up to us to exhibit workstyles that honor God.

It's not easy to work for Christ . . . but it is well worth it. And the retirement plan? Well, it's out of this world!

LEADER'S GUIDE TO
MAKING YOUR WORK COUNT FOR GOD

This workbook has been prepared primarily for individual study. Nevertheless, it lends itself quite easily to group study and discussion. Because of the personal nature of many of the questions, it is recommended that each member of your group has a workbook to ensure privacy.

You don't need to be a Bible scholar or a motivational speaker to lead a study group. All you need to do is follow the format established in each chapter. The material included in this Leader's Guide is intended to be a supplement for each lesson, not a substitute.

Here are a few suggestions for forming and leading a study group:

1. Your group may be composed of men and women of varying ages. It may be an existing Bible study group, a Sunday school class, or a lunchtime gathering in your workplace. Ideally, the group should not be larger than twelve people. The larger the group is, the more difficult it will be for you to "direct traffic" and keep the discussion focused on the subject.

2. Assign the first chapter to your group and explain that you will be discussing only one chapter each week for the next twelve weeks. Encourage group members to read each article carefully, and answer all questions as thoroughly as possible before coming to class. If there are words, concepts, or Scripture passages a group member does not understand, that person should make note of that in the workbook. These subjects can be addressed during group discussions.

3. Your job as the leader is not to be the "answer person." Your role is to facilitate the discussions. When you introduce the session, be sure to point out that for many of the questions there are no right or wrong answers.

4. Open each class by welcoming everyone. Be sure to greet new members of the group. You may want to share any stories of events from the previous week. If desired, you can open the session with a prayer.

5. Next, you could do a brief review of the previous session. For the first class you may want to begin with the introduction to this workbook. Next you will want to introduce the new lesson. This would be the time to present the objectives for the session. You may want to list them on a chalkboard.

6. One way to begin the discussion is by reading one of the stories or an article in the chapter. The questions listed in this Leader's Guide address the main points of the chapter. If the group wants to focus on a particular issue, feel free to review the relevant articles, Scripture, and questions in more detail. The key to having a successful discussion is getting the group involved; it is not critical to try to work through every question listed. Encourage personal testimonies of how God is using the members of your group in the workplace, but limit the testimony time to three minutes.

7. In some lessons, it may be helpful to read aloud portions of an article, but be sensitive

to those members of your group who may be embarrassed about reading in front of other people. If you have any reason to think someone would feel awkward, read the material aloud yourself.

Also, be aware of anyone who is not taking an active role in the group. If someone is not participating, give that person an opportunity to contribute by saying, "Bob, would you like to share your answer to question two?" If that person appears nervous or uncomfortable answering in front of the group, do not push for an answer. Some people do not like to speak in front of a group. On the other hand, you may have a person who jumps to answer every question, not giving the others a chance to participate. One way to handle this is to say, "That's a good point. Anyone else?"

8. If you complete the questions in the Leader's Guide before the session is over, you can focus on the more specific questions in the chapter. Perhaps a point was made earlier in the session that warrants further discussion. If you come to a question that does not spark much discussion, move on.

9. Some individuals may have specific questions from when they worked through the chapter prior to the session. Encourage everyone to bring up specific questions during the discussion time.

10. At the end of each session, ask the group members to study the next chapter on their own before the next session. Encourage members to pray specifically for each other during the upcoming week. Close the session with a brief prayer of thanksgiving or another appropriate prayer.

11. For a fifty-minute session, allow seven minutes for the welcome and warm-up. Take three minutes to review the previous session. Introduce the new lesson in five minutes. Allow thirty minutes for discussion of this week's chapter, and leave five minutes for closing discussion.

Chapter 1: "But It's Just *Work*"

As you better understand how highly God values your work, you will find a sense of purpose that far surpasses the satisfaction you receive from getting a paycheck, or even the "warm fuzzies" you feel when you receive the appreciation of your superiors or the respect of your peers. Knowing that your work matters to God gives you that extra incentive to get out of bed each morning.

You are not merely making a living. You are faithfully managing the resources and responsibilities that God has placed under your control. Service replaces selfishness as your motivation for what you do. Since you represent Jesus in your workplace, you have an even greater responsibility to do honest, quality work.

Lesson Objectives

1. *To examine some of the more commonly held workplace myths, mistakes, and unbiblical concepts about work.*
2. *To see how your work is an extension of God's rule in the world.*
3. *To show that God does not differentiate between "church work" and "secular work."*
4. *To show that God cares more about your character and conduct than your occupational status.*

Discuss

1. Are there some types of work that God does not regard as legitimate? How do you think God views your work?
2. See the article "Workplace Myths" and 1 Corinthians 3:5–9 on pages 2–4. Discuss the tendency to put ministers and missionaries on a pedestal because of the type of work they do. Why do we do this? What is wrong with doing this?
3. What does Paul mean by saying that "we are God's fellow workers" (1 Cor. 3:9) on page 4?
4. See 1 Corinthians 12:15–31 and the article "Are Some Jobs More Important than Others?" on pages 13–14. What are some specific ways your living out "the more excellent way" (verse 31) might make a difference in your character and conduct in the workplace?

Chapter 2: A Commitment to Excellence

The apostle Paul recognized that it was necessary for somebody to be giving orders and for someone to be taking them. As a result, he instructs us to have a mutual respect for each other. Whether you are a boss in authority or a worker under authority, employees and employers are ultimately under the authority of Christ.

In our effort to serve God and please Him, we strive to do our best. Sometimes our coworkers do not appreciate our commitment to excellence and they develop a competitive attitude toward us. Usually, the cause of such needless conflict comes down to a simple question: Who gets the credit for a job well done, or the blame when the job is botched?

Our integrity will be challenged in the workplace. We must consider how our work habits influence our reputations. Consider the song lyrics on page 29. It is such inconsistencies that will trip us up every time. Usually it's not the "big sins" that destroy a believer's integrity. More often it is something small and seemingly insignificant that creates the contradictions regarding the validity of our Christian faith and lifestyle.

Lesson Objectives

1. To show that Christ is our ultimate boss and that all work should be done with the attitude that we are working for Him.
2. To explore standards of fairness between labor and management.
3. To see why it doesn't matter who gets the credit. God desires cooperation among coworkers rather than competition.
4. To encourage integrity in our work habits.

Discuss

1. Read the article "Who's the Boss?" and the accompanying Scripture (Col. 3:22–24) on pages 18–19. How does the idea that Christ is your ultimate Boss affect your workstyle and your attitude about your work?

2. According to the article "Who Gets the Credit?" on page 22, God desires cooperation, not competition, among His people. How can competition be healthy in sports, for example, but often destructive in the workplace?
3. According to "Your 'Workstyle' " and Titus 2:9–10 on pages 30–31, your attitudes and actions at work can present the gospel in a positive or negative way to coworkers and customers. What impression are you making?

Chapter 3: More than Words

Witnessing for Christ is telling other people what Jesus means to you and what He can do for them. Is it possible to be an effective witness for Jesus in the workplace without losing your job, your friends, or your sanity? Yes, it is! But many Christians are reluctant to say anything about their faith in Christ, especially in the workplace.

To earn the right to be heard, you need to present evidence of a Christian workstyle before presenting others with mere information. As you model authentic Christianity by doing your work conscientiously and by genuinely caring about your coworkers, opportunities will open for you to discuss the gospel.

One difficulty in sharing Jesus with your coworkers is trying to communicate the message in a language and manner they can understand. By meeting others on their level and by demonstrating a Christlike lifestyle, you will have a better chance of reaching others.

Lesson Objectives

1. *To see why Christians ought to be the best employees in the workplace.*
2. *To understand that believers must earn the right to be heard within the workplace by demonstrating a Christian workstyle.*
3. *To learn to communicate the message of Christ in a way your coworkers will most easily understand.*

Discuss

1. Look at 1 Timothy 6:1–2 on page 34. According to this passage, why is the idea of a Christian's cheating or manipulating an employer so unacceptable?
2. Review "Work—A Platform for Evangelism" on page 36 and the accompanying Scripture. What does Paul mean when he challenges us to work with "sincerity of heart"?
3. Ephesians 6:6 (page 37) implies that by applying yourself in the workplace you are "doing the will of God." What are some specific ways you can do God's will in your workplace?
4. How did the apostle Paul seek to build bridges into the lives of his listeners in each of the accounts noted in the article "Audience-shaped Messages" on pages 43–44?

Chapter 4: Don't Discount Diversity

It takes courage to cross cultural barriers within the workplace. Some of your coworkers may not understand your actions or they may misinterpret your motives. But the risk will be worth it. After all, if anyone should lead the way in breaking down barriers established by prejudice, it is the believer. Don't be afraid to take the first step along "the road less traveled." Jesus will meet you there and will walk with you every step of the way.

If we commit ourselves to Christ and repent of any prejudice we may have, then God will revitalize our spiritual lives. He will also give us a fresh understanding of His desire to bring people of every background into His family. That in itself should motivate us to tear down walls that divide. As we begin to actively build bridges to those who are different from us, we will discover that what binds us together as believers is stronger than what divides us.

Lesson Objectives

1. To examine how Jesus sets an example of overcoming prejudice by speaking to the Samaritan woman.
2. To see that God can cause things that are intended to be barriers to the gospel can become open doors.
3. To understand how the gospel is for all people.

Discuss

1. In John 4:4–42, Jesus dispelled the prejudice surrounding the Samaritan woman (pages 50–51). What patterns do you see in Jesus' encounter with this woman that might help you dispel prejudice in your workplace?
2. What kinds of rivalries or tensions currently exist within your workplace? What can you do to help remove these barriers?
3. Look at "Ethnic Walls Break Down" and Acts 10:1–48 on pages 58–61. How did God use the visions of the unclean animals to convince Peter to break down ethnic walls? Why didn't God send Philip to take the gospel to Cornelius?
4. In Revelation 7:14 (page 63), we are told who makes up the great multitude before God's throne. Who are these people?
5. How does knowing that you will spend eternity with people from every race, culture, and ethnic background affect your attitude toward those who are different from you?

Chapter 5: At Work in Your City

We may not realize it, but God loves cities! Human history may have begun in a garden, but it will end in a city—God's city. In the meantime, we must learn to live and work in an environment that is extremely different from that in which we may have grown up. We must learn how to cross cultural lines to share our faith in Jesus.

As we become more aware of and involved in our world, we learn that there are many hardships. Many of us become apathetic because we are overwhelmed by all the problems in society. We wonder what we, as individuals, can possibly do to make a difference in the world. But we can each make a difference if we simply take the first step. Jesus made a point of reaching out to people that society had rejected, ignored, or ostracized. These folks listened to Him gladly, and they still do today.

Lesson Objectives

1. To see how our society is becoming more of an urban society, and that Jesus expects us to minister to it.
2. To remind us that Jesus ministered to people one-on-one, not just to the masses.
3. To learn how we can take the gospel to those who are hurting and impoverished.
4. To discover what made Antioch a thriving center for early Christianity and how we can emulate that model.

Discuss

1. We are told in "Jesus—A City Preacher" on page 66 that Jesus sent the disciples to the cities to preach. Why do you think He did that?
2. How can you make your neighborhood a better place to live?
3. Hundreds of needs were represented in the crowd in Mark 5:21–43 (page 70), yet, as far as we know, Jesus healed only two individuals. What do Jesus' actions tell us about the people who are sent our way?
4. How can your concern (or lack of concern) about society's underclass impact welfare and other government programs? (See "The Underclass" on page 73.)
5. Look at the article "Antioch: A Model for the Modern Church?" (pages 75–76) and notice the four keys to their success. Now, let's assume that you are a manager attempting to motivate your employees and create a greater sense of camaraderie in your workplace. Create a four-point plan that might help you accomplish your goal.

Chapter 6: What Is True Success?

What is God's idea of success? Despite society's belief, it is not wealth, power, prestige, or fame. The Bible promises a reward to believers who gauge their success by God's standards and seek to please Him. When you follow God's standards, you may or may not be rewarded in this life. However, you will be rewarded in heaven.

Can a Christian be successful in this world? Certainly! But where the world's idea of success clashes with true success, the believer must be ready to willingly place everything in the hands of Christ. Furthermore, every believer has a responsibility to use the gifts, talents, and resources of God for His glory.

Lesson Objectives

1. *To show that God's ideas regarding true success are radically different from society's.*
2. *To discover why success in the workplace is useless if we harm our relationship with God.*
3. *To see how we can faithfully use the gifts and resources God has granted us.*
4. *To show the value of observing the Sabbath by resting, relaxing, and focusing on your relationship with God and your family.*

Discuss

1. How do you define success? Review the article "Success" on pages 82–83. Who sets the standards by which you measure success? What price are you willing to pay in order to achieve success?
2. John the Baptist's idea of success was to point people to Jesus, which is why he said, "He must increase, but I must decrease" (John 3:30, page 81). What is your primary motive for pursuing success?
3. In Matthew 25:15 (page 86), notice that the master gave the men talents "each according to his own ability." What reasons could a person have for not faithfully using what he was given?
4. In Luke 9:25 (page 89), Jesus asks, "What profit is it to a man if he gains the whole world, and is himself destroyed or lost?" What does this mean?
5. God did not create you to be a perpetual motion machine. He intends for you to observe the Sabbath as a day of rest and restoration. How would observing the Sabbath improve your attitude toward your work? (See "Why Not Rest a While" on page 91.)

Chapter 7: You're Not the Lone Ranger

Accountability. For many of us it is the missing ingredient in our spiritual lives. After all, most of us don't like to have anyone looking over our shoulders and keeping track of how we're doing. But God never intended for us to function as Spiritual Lone Rangers. Most of us need someone who loves us enough to look us in the eyes and say, "I think you're getting off track." There is strength and security in knowing that someone who loves us is watching out for us.

The Bible clearly establishes the fact that we must be accountable for our actions and attitudes, as well as for the possessions, wealth, and time that God has given to us. Most of the accountability issues boil down to one central question: What are you doing with what God has given you?

Lesson Objectives

1. *To understand why we need to be accountable to each other, as well as to God.*
2. *To see how we are accountable not just for what we do with our possessions, but also for how we treat the people with whom we live and work.*
3. *To discover why we are accountable to God for how we prioritize our time.*

Discuss

1. Look at the article "Accountability" on page 94. What three principles of accountability are discussed, and how can adopting these principles strengthen your relationship with God?
2. In Acts 16:16–24 (page 97), we read about a slave girl whose masters were exploiting her for their own profits. What are some contemporary examples in which you believe employers are exploiting their employees? (Your examples do not have to be from your workplace.) What can you do about these situations?
3. Review the article on pages 99–100, "Owners or Tenants." Imagine that all your possessions are borrowed, and you will have to return them soon. When you return them, you will have to tell the owner how the items were used. What would you say?
4. In Luke 18:35–43 (pages 102–103) we are told of a blind beggar who called out to Jesus from the roadside. Why do you suppose the people around Jesus tried to quiet the beggar and keep him away from Jesus? Why did Jesus stop to help the man?

Chapter 8: Money, Money, and More Money!

Few things impact our lives as much as the "almighty dollar." For most of us it determines where we live, where we work, what we do with our time, where (or if) we go on vacation, and when and where we will retire. Money is more than a means of exchange. In many ways, your money is you. How you make your money and how you spend or save it are some of the clearest indicators in your life regarding your priorities and commitments.

Money pressures can place an enormous strain on even the best relationships at work and at home. But God wants you to control your money, instead of letting your money control you. Money never satisfies. If your reason for working so hard is "to keep up with the Joneses," you are on a destructive path. Furthermore, if you are working at an unfulfilling job, hoping that greater financial gain will compensate for your unhappiness, you will inevitably be disappointed. Money and materialism can never deliver true satisfaction.

Lesson Objectives

1. To show that we do not work because of greed. We work to honor God.
2. To show that it is possible to have a lifestyle of contentment, whether you are rich or poor.
3. To understand how "prosperity theology" perverts God's message that we reap what we sow.
4. To show the obstacles a rich person must overcome if he wants to enter the kingdom of God. The account of the rich young ruler is used to illustrate this truth.

Discuss

1. If you had enough money to live comfortably for the rest of your life, what work would you do, if any?
2. It is mentioned in "Christians and Money" (pages 106–107) that "people who love money

are vulnerable to all kinds of evil." What are some of those evils, and what does the apostle Paul say is the worst of these evils?

3. In Paul's instructions to Timothy (vv. 11–16, pages 107–108), the apostle implies that contentment can be learned. What are some things you can do to help develop contentment?

4. Review the article "The Dangers of Prosperity Theology" on pages 109–110. God promises to supply everything you need, and He promises that you will reap according to how you sow. Yet, "prosperity theology" often perverts God's meaning. Where is the balance? What factors make the difference?

5. What do you think Jesus meant when He said it was hard for a rich person to enter the kingdom of God? (See Mark 10:17–27, page 112.)

Chapter 9: People Power

The making of disciples and being a mentor to them was a priority for Jesus. Likewise, it must be a priority for us. Since the most effective mentoring relationships involve people with whom you have regular contact, it is only natural to seek out such a relationship with a coworker.

True mentors lead by example. They understand one of the most elementary lessons of leadership, which is often overlooked. Leadership is not a position of privilege, but one of service.

Kingdom-style mentors willingly convey to their coworkers the wisdom, knowledge, and skills they have developed, and even rejoice when their understudies experience greater success than the mentor. Mentors must not be afraid of confrontation, though; they must be willing to correct their followers when they are in error. Eventually the follower can become a mentor himself.

Lesson Objectives

1. *To show the need, value, and biblical pattern of mentoring.*
2. *To realize that even Jesus sought and submitted to wise teaching.*
3. *To show that mentors are servant-leaders.*
4. *To encourage leaders (at work and at home) to delegate responsibilities to others and to allow them the freedom to follow through with the job, even if they don't do it as well as you think they should.*

Discuss

1. Look at the article "Mentoring, Kingdom-Style" on page 116. What pattern do you see of older believers working with younger ones?
2. "Jesus the Student" (page 119) tells us that we need to learn all we can from the best teachers we can find. How did Jesus, at age twelve, demonstrate this when He was in the temple?
3. Hebrews 5:1–14 (pages 122–123) describes Jesus as the perfect priest who served His

people. What qualities or principles can you find in Christ's example that provide a model for mentors?
4. In Luke 10:1 (page 125), why do you think Jesus delegated His work to seventy other workers rather than doing it Himself? Why do you think many people are reluctant to delegate responsibilities?

Chapter 10: Working on the Family Front

If you work outside your home (as most people do for at least part of their lives), you will probably spend almost as much time in the workplace as you do with your family. Conflicts between home and work responsibilities are inevitable.

Family conflicts, past and present, cause great tension for all those involved. Whatever the source of the conflict is, the real issue is whether or not you are going to allow these issues to destroy your family life. Your relationship with your family members can be strengthened and restored through love and forgiveness. After a person's relationship with Christ, marriage and family are meant to be the most intimate and fulfilling relationships you can have.

Lesson Objectives

1. *To emphasize that the family relationship is primary to the believer through all phases of life.*
2. *To show that commitment makes all the difference when it comes to family relationships.*
3. *To discover that despite horrendous societal pressures aimed at tearing our families apart, there is hope for the family because it is a priority for God.*

Discuss

1. Look at the article "The Family: A Call to Long-Term Work" on pages 128–129. Where is your family among the six phases of family life?
2. What are some things you can do to lessen the tension between your family and work?
3. Why are there so many conflicts within families? How can we guard against a negative outcome from such conflicts? (See "For or Against Family?" on pages 131–132.)
4. In Matthew 19:1–15 (page 134), it is easy to see that Jesus saw marriage as a permanent commitment, not a relationship of convenience. What mistakes did the disciples make in their understanding of the Old Testament laws concerning divorce?
5. What struggles are you currently experiencing in your family? How can Revelation 19:6–10 (page 137) bolster your faith in the fact that Jesus will bring you through these situations victoriously? (See "There Is Hope for the Family" on pages 136–137.)

Chapter 11: Taking Your Convictions to Work

Being a Christian is not as simple as following a long list of rules. There will be many times when we are faced with situations that call for us to make decisions based on what we think will honor God. The tough part is that there isn't always one answer to a question.

God does not expect each of us to look, act, or think in exactly the same way. Because of this, there can be more than one way to resolve difficult issues and still please God. He does, however, expect us to be people of integrity who follow our convictions. He also expects us to accept those whose convictions are different from ours.

Lesson Objectives

1. *To emphasize the need for honesty and integrity on the part of believers in the workplace.*
2. *To show that equally devout believers differ in their opinions regarding matters of conscience or personal convictions. How are we to judge?*
3. *To discover the power of the gospel in healing relationships and resolving grievances among believers. Paul's wise dealings with Philemon and Onesimus are used as an illustration.*
4. *To discover what Jesus meant when He said we should "judge all things" (1 Cor. 2:15).*

Discuss

1. What does Paul mean when he says we should be blameless, harmless, and without fault? (See Philippians 2:14–16 on page 140.)
2. The article "Honesty and Ethical Standards" on page 139 says that many occupations are thought to have decreasing ethics and standards of honesty. How can we change this perception?
3. What is the difference between judging and condemning?
4. Are we to judge all things? Discuss the article on pages 143–144.
5. In Romans 14:1–12 (page 146), Paul lists at least four reasons why believers should accept one another, despite their differences. What are these reasons?
6. What price was Paul willing to pay in order to see the reconciliation between Philemon and Onesimus (Philemon 8–21, page 151)? What sacrifices are you willing to make in order to aid in the healing of relationships of your coworkers?

Chapter 12: Tackling Times of Trial

Jesus never said it would be easy to follow Him. Nor did He imply that you would be popular for wanting to represent Him in the workplace. But Christ did promise that no one would ever serve Him in vain.

There will always be stresses, trials, and tribulations in the workplace. Competitiveness and jealousy may be directed toward you for no apparent reason. Nevertheless, as you continue to respond with grace, kindness, and love, God will give you the strength you need to overcome the trials, and He will even bring good out of what may have been intended for evil. Through your trials, God will continue to teach you, getting you ready to spend eternity with Him.

Lesson Objectives

1. *To understand why there will be a price to pay for following Christ. In the workplace, we can expect to face some opposition.*

2. *To show how the believer's commitment to personal integrity will result in eternal dividends.*
3. *To see how God uses trials to develop our patience and wisdom.*

Discuss

1. As long as we live as God's people on this earth, we can expect a connection between trouble and hope. (See "Welcome to Stressful Living" on pages 153–154.) What kinds of troubles have you experienced lately, especially at work? How can you (or have you) grow from these experiences?
2. How is it possible for you to "count it all joy" (James 1:2, page 156) when troubles come?
3. Look at "Retaliation Foiled" and Luke 20:20–26 on pages 157–158. Why do you think the spies' inquiry to Jesus regarding taxes was such a loaded question? How did Jesus foil the efforts of His enemies and still teach an important lesson on priorities?
4. Romans 8:28 (page 161) tells us that "all things work together for good to those who love God." How can the faith that God will work all things together for your ultimate good give you confidence in the workplace?

Chapter 13: Take This Job and . . . Love It!

This chapter is intended to help participants sum up what they've learned so they can put it to use in daily life. It consists of summaries of the first twelve chapters and questions that highlight the main points. You could use the material as a review by working through the entire chapter. This may take a couple of weeks, depending on the size of your group. If you want to review all twelve chapters at one time, you would be limited to spending a maximum of four minutes on each chapter.

If you do not have enough time to do the whole chapter, you could review chapter 13 before your group meets and select the questions you think will be most helpful for your group. You should encourage members to do chapter 13 on their own because it will reinforce what each one has learned.

The main point to stress to your group is that work is not a meaningless way to pass the time. Our work matters to God; He cares about what we do and how we do it. However, our work does not determine our value as people. Our lives have innate value to God. We may not be able to change certain unpleasant circumstances in the workplace, but we can change our attitudes and actions. It is up to us to exhibit workstyles that honor God. It's not easy to work for God, but it is well worth it!